Kenneth Copeland Ministries

Presents this Special Partner Edition of

Dear Partner

to

_____

on this day of _____ 19_____ ,

to commemorate our Covenant of Partnership
together. Gloria and I are committed to minister to you,
to pray for you every day, and to continue teaching you
the uncompromised Word of God that you may
continue to grow and increase in His anointing.
We stand with you in faith, and we love you.

Kenneth Copeland

Kenneth Copeland

Dear Partner

KCP

Kenneth Copeland Publications
Fort Worth, Texas

Dear Partner

ISBN 1-57562-148-7   30-0049

All scripture is from the *King James Version* unless otherwise noted.

Kenneth Copeland Publications
Fort Worth, Texas 76192-0001

To My Partners...

Grace be unto you, and peace, from God our Father,
and from the Lord Jesus Christ.
I thank my God upon every remembrance of you,
Always in every prayer of mine for you all
making request with joy,
For your partnership in the gospel
from the first day until now;
Being confident of this very thing,
that he which hath begun a good work in you
will perform it until the day of Jesus Christ:
Even as it is meet for me to think this of you all,
because I have you in my heart;
inasmuch as both in my bonds,
and in the defence and confirmation of the gospel,
ye all are partakers of my grace (Philippians 1:2-7).

Kenneth

Table of Contents

February 1986

Letters of Faith

Dear Partner,

Recently the Lord has given me a new and deeper calling to minister directly to you, my Covenant Partner, through my letters to you. In the light of God's Word, I've seen those letters in a new and powerful way. And no matter how much of my time and prayer it takes, I'm going to do my very best to get an anointed, faith-filled letter to you each month to help you live that month in greater victory. This is my commitment to you.

Ever since the Church began, letters have been a powerful tool in God's hand. He entrusted His precious gospel to be communicated by letters. These letters by Paul, John, Luke and others carried the Word of His Power to His people. They still do.

In Paul's letters, he referred to the times he spent in prayer for the people and then wrote by inspiration of the Holy Spirit. That means the letters of Paul and the others God inspired to write are the Holy Scriptures. The letters you will receive from me will always be based on and subject to those inspired letters of God's eternal Word. As I intercede in prayer for you, I expect the Holy Spirit to anoint me with an anointing that is greater than your needs. Out of that anointing will come my letters to you.

So pay close attention to them. Treat them with great respect, for the anointing will be on them. After they have ministered to you, don't just forget about them. Continue to think on them. Give God the opportunity to continue to use them in your life as seeds of my faith for your prosperity.

You have my word, that everything I say I will do for you in these letters, I will *actually* do! You know I'll keep my word.

I'm working on your next letter now. I am charged with God's power. Be expecting it. I can hardly wait for you to read it. I believe it will be almost like talking face to face. Until then, remember that Gloria and I love you—and Jesus is Lord!

Your Covenant Partner,
Kenneth Copeland

April 1986

The Keys Are Coming!

Dear Partner,

Have you ever been in a situation where, no matter how hard you tried, there just wasn't any way out? Every direction you looked you saw the same answer—*none at all!?*

You may be in the middle of something like that right now. I've been in that kind of spiritual box canyon more than once, and the Holy Spirit has taught me a Bible faith principle of deliverance that I believe will help you receive your miracles when you need them. So study what I'm about to share with you carefully.

Let's begin by looking at Matthew 16:19: *"And I will give unto thee the keys of the kingdom of heaven: and whatsoever thou shalt bind on earth shall be bound in heaven: and whatsoever thou shalt loose on earth shall be loosed in heaven."*

Everything has a key! Did you know that?

There is no problem so carefully planned by the forces of darkness that the kingdom of God does not have a key that will unlock it and solve it with kingdom power. Every situation has a key issue, a vital spot, that is important to you as a target for your faith.

You can see an example of that in Matthew 14:28-30. There, Peter, who had just seen Jesus walking on the water, had called out to Him and said, *"Lord, if it be thou, bid me*

*come unto thee on the water. And he [Jesus] said, Come.
And when Peter was come down out of the ship, he walked
on the water, to go to Jesus. But when he saw the wind
boisterous, he was afraid; and beginning to sink, he cried,
saying, Lord, save me."*

Now, what happened in that situation? What caused
Peter to stop walking and start sinking?

Without realizing it, Peter took his eyes off the key issue—
Jesus' word. What was the word? *"Come."* Peter suddenly
thought the key issue was the wind. It wasn't. The wind had
nothing to do with his being able to walk on the water.

In Luke 6:46-49 we see a similar example in Jesus' parable about the men who built their houses, one on rock, and
the other on sand. Let's read it:

**[46]Why call ye me, Lord, Lord, and do not the
things which I say?**

**[47]Whosoever cometh to me, and heareth my
sayings, and doeth them, I will show you to
whom he is like:**

**[48]He is like a man which built an house, and
digged deep, and laid the foundation on a rock:
and when the flood arose, the stream beat
vehemently upon that house, and could not
shake it: for it was founded upon a rock.**

**[49]But he that heareth, and doeth not, is like a
man that without a foundation built an house
upon the earth; against which the stream did
beat vehemently, and immediately it fell; and
the ruin of that house was great.**

Notice the key issue there. It may first appear that the storm destroyed the house. But the storm wasn't the real problem. If it were, it would have destroyed *both* houses. The key issue was the foundation.

By determining the key issue and applying your faith, you can turn *any* situation in your life around!

Let me show you what I mean. Years ago, there was a time when our ministry was $1 million in the red. When I first went to God in prayer about the situation, I was convinced that the money to pay off that deficit was what I needed. But as I prayed and sought God for the key, He instructed me to begin giving the top 10 percent of our income into ministry for the poor.

You see, the money I needed was a side issue—not the key. The key issue was the ministry to the poor. Had God just provided the money, the problem that allowed the devil to steal from us would have still been there. Even if we'd paid that million-dollar deficit off, we'd have still been in trouble. We probably would have ended the next year even further behind!

Instead, we began to better understand how to change and improve what we were doing. We were not only delivered from the deficit, but gave 10 percent more than ever before—all on the same yearly income! We found the key issue!

Every situation has a key.

As you pray for members of your family and friends, you need to realize there is a key to every person's salvation and healing. That key may be a special scripture or a special thought from God. It may be a particular person who can speak to them in a way they can more fully understand. That's why it's so important to pray according to the Word that says, *"Pray ye therefore the Lord of the harvest, that he will send forth labourers into his harvest"* (Matthew 9:38). God holds the key to every person.

Start praying in faith now that God will reveal the keys you need to unlock your situation.

I know there are things that need to be completed in your life—things you've been standing in faith for that need to come on through. Well, I'm setting myself in faith with you now, that in Jesus' mighty Name you'll receive the kingdom keys that will unlock God's truth. His miracle power will lock the devil up tight.

Now is the time to rise up together like champions of faith!

There comes the moment when champions rise up and seize the victory. It's the fourth-quarter drive, the ninth-inning surge, the great invasion into enemy territory that wins the war. This is that moment! I am releasing my faith now to help you get the kingdom keys you need to rise up and overcome!

Here's what I want you to do.

1. Write down the situations in which you need kingdom keys revealed to you.

2. Pray and ask God to reveal to you what He would have you do about planting seeds in His kingdom.

3. Lay your hands on your seed and declare it planted. Once it's planted in faith, you're in a position to receive.

Wrap your seed in words of faith. Say out loud, "It is finished! I have the key!"
Take heart, your keys are coming!

Your Brother and Partner in Jesus' Service,
Kenneth

May 1986

We Need One Another!

Dear Partner,

I never knew you could feel so close to someone and not actually be in their presence. God is performing a miracle bond between you and me that I believe is something special.

You're an important part of my life. I deeply appreciate your prayers and your gifts for me and this ministry. As Paul said, I may not be with you in the flesh, but I am with you in the Spirit. Together, we are entering into what Jesus prayed in John 17:21: *"That they all may be one; as thou, Father, art in me, and I in thee, that they also may be one in us: that the world may believe that thou hast sent me."*

You and I must set an example of believers holding on to one another in good times as well as bad. We need one another! I need your faith as much as you need mine. Together, we can face anything, expecting victory in Jesus to come through triumphantly.

God's Word in John 3:34 says Jesus was given the Holy Spirit without measure. He defeated all of hell without any assistance. More powerful than all the demons of hell and all the wicked spirits of all classes—including Satan himself—Jesus was able to defeat their combined power. He made an open show of them, triumphing over them (Colossians 2:15).

I said all that to say this: We are His Body. Each of us has been given the measure of faith according to Romans 12:1-3. That is enough to take care of our personal needs. However, there is more involved here than just our personal lives.

We are the end-time generation. We are the "terrorism" generation. We are the people who need more of God's power in our midst than any other generation before us.

We need all the help we can get! But thank God, we can get all the help we need!

The scripture says one of us can put a thousand to flight and two of us together can put 10,000 to flight. There's a very definite spiritual law that activates when we come together, and increases the measure of our spiritual strength to the 10th power. That means only four of us are more powerful in God than 10 million evil spirits. Only two of us, like you and me, in agreement prayer can move the very heart of our Father God (Matthew 18:19-20).

Take a look at Ephesians 4:13. Read it slowly and carefully. *"Till we all come in the unity of the faith, and of the knowledge of the Son of God, unto a perfect man, unto the measure of the stature of the fulness of Christ."*

Take special note of the word *measure.* When the Body of Christ comes together and begins to function as one, we will have the Holy Spirit *without measure!*

We will begin to see ministries functioning in the fullness of their callings. We will begin to see manifestations of the Holy Spirit in full measure. We will see Jesus in fullness of stature as we've never seen Him before. Then the world will know that the Father sent Him.

All this has to start with you and me holding on to one

another in faith and love. Let's make a daily effort to make ourselves available to God to pray. Start your day by saying, *"Holy Spirit, use me to pray for someone today. I offer You my measure of faith."*

I start my day praying like that. Think about what would happen if all of us joined together in prayer. When you prayed for me, you'd actually be praying for the whole Body of Christ because *we are one.*

I believe our daily prayers for each other will get the same kind of powerful results. They will help us join our faith together and increase our measure of Holy Ghost power, not just from the two of us, but from thousands of us. All the demons of hell can't overcome us when we get together. We are more than conquerors!

I believe we will rise up and go over the top. I'm lifting you up with my faith as you lift me with yours.

Gloria and I love and appreciate you.

Your Brother and Partner in Jesus' Service,
Kenneth

June 1986

Look Up!

Dear Partner,

When God first planted the seeds of this letter in my heart, I was in Johannesburg, South Africa. I'd been seeing a wave of revival there that you can hardly imagine.

I wish you could have been with me to see it yourself. People there were being swept into the kingdom of God in unprecedented numbers. Miracles were happening everywhere—in the churches, on the streets, in places of business. It beat all I had ever seen.

But in the middle of all the excitement, I still found myself thinking about you. In fact, I woke up one night praying for you, and for all my other friends like you who do so much to help me in this ministry.

At first, I wasn't sure what I was praying about. I only knew the need was urgent and two hours later I began to know why. The Lord showed me a spirit of weariness was trying to work its way into all of our lives through all the pressure and the bad news that surrounds us.

That's why I'm writing you today. I want to tell you what the Lord told me that night in Johannesburg. And I want to encourage you to *look up*...because in times like these, your very life may depend on it.

You see, we are constantly being bombarded by negative

forces that are working to divert our eyes from the positive faith of the Word of God. When we yield to those forces, our spirit man begins to weaken. The Word lets us know what the result is: You will *"be wearied and faint in your minds"* (Hebrews 12:3). Beware of that weariness!

Jesus said in Mark 4:19 that the cares of this world, entering in, will choke the Word and cause it to become unfruitful. Your faith, remember, is a fruit of the Word. You absolutely cannot afford to be without your faith.

Can you see how one thing leads to another? As we allow the negative circumstances to distract us from the Word of God, we become weak and weary. Then our faith begins to wither. And without faith, we're headed for disaster.

What can we do to stop this chain reaction of weariness?

First—Look up! Get your eyes back on Jesus. I remember on the field of athletic competition that when an opponent allowed himself to drop his head, he became very easily defeated. He was no longer dangerous to my victory.

Hebrews 12:2-3, once again, says to consider Jesus, the Author and Finisher of our faith Who is now at the right hand of the throne of God. Consider Him, instead of the cares of this world. Look up!

Second—Get back into the Word. Be more faithful to the Word of God than to the news broadcasts, the newspapers and the bad-news friends who constantly talk about what the devil is doing. Remember Romans 10:17: *"Faith cometh by hearing and hearing by the Word of God."* Get into the Word!

Third—Don't be afraid that you're going to lose everything. God is your source, not the world. He can take care of you regardless of what happens around you. Fear not!

Fourth—Don't be weary in well-doing for *"in due season we shall reap, if we faint not"* (Galatians 6:9). And we will not faint if we consider Him.

So, begin a new cycle by keeping your eyes on Jesus. Then Satan cannot steal the Word. Then the Word's fruit—your faith—will be strong. Then you can please God. Then whatsoever you ask of Him, you will receive (1 John 3:22).

Now the chain reaction is working for you instead of against you—all because you made one adjustment first. You began to lift up your eyes. You began to raise up your head instead of looking down. God is up. Jesus is up. The devil is down—*under your feet!*

Always remember, you are not alone. I pray for you every day. My prayers and the prayers of the thousands of other believers who are working together with us through this ministry are all pulling together for all our success.

Your gifts and prayers are joining with other gifts and prayers of faith to create a river of power that is setting people free all over the world. I'm telling you it's working! Satan's strongholds are being torn down. Don't let up on him now. Keep believing God and planting seeds of faith and giving.

Look up! Your harvest is coming.

I thank God upon every remembrance of you. You are always in my heart.

> Your Friend and Partner in Jesus' Service,
> Kenneth

September 1986

Today Could Be the Day of Your Breakthrough

Dear Partner,

I know that you know the Lord as Savior. You know Him as your Helper, your Guide, and your comfort in times of trouble. You know Him as your Covenant Brother.

In this letter, I want you to get to know Him in a new and powerful way. I want you to know Him as *"The Lord of the Breakthrough!"*

There is a story in 1 Chronicles 14:8-17 about a time when the Philistine army rose up against King David. When he prayed about whether or not he should go fight against them, God told him, *"Go. I will deliver them into your hand."*

If you'll read the account, you'll find that in the 11th verse, David said something very interesting about his victory. He said, *"God hath broken in upon mine enemies by mine hand like the breaking forth of waters...."*

Do you remember the old story about the little boy who found a small leak in the back of a dam? The dam was holding back a large body of water. So, the boy stuck his finger in the small hole and held it until help could come and repair the dam.

What was the big deal about such a small hole? How could only one hole be so important?

Because that one little, leaky hole would gradually grow until suddenly there was a breakthrough! Then the flood could not be stopped. In the light of that illustration, let's look again at 1 Chronicles 14:11: *"So they came up to Baal-perazim; and David smote them there. Then David said, God hath broken in upon mine enemies by mine hand like the breaking forth of waters: therefore they called the name of that place Baal-perazim."* (Baal-perazim literally translated means *Lord of the Breakthrough*. One translation says, "The Master of the Breakthrough.")

Now think again for a moment about the small hole in the dam. Picture in your mind all the water on the other side. Think about the tremendous pressure that was being applied to that one little hole.

God's power is applying pressure to the dam Satan has built up before you. It's ready to push through for you.

The breakthrough will come if you'll pray and stand against the devil. You don't have to push over the entire dam. All you have to do is get a small hole started. Once you do that, don't give up and don't quit. It's when you give up that Satan has a chance to patch the hole. *So, don't quit!*

Keep being the very best you can be. Keep being positive. Pray a little longer. Stay in the Word. Walk by faith and not by sight. Walk by faith and not by feelings.

Keep walking in love regardless of what anyone else does or says. Don't let yourself be hurt and wounded over what people say or do. Don't give up on your healing. Your miracle breakthrough is about to happen.

Keep planting seed. Keep watering that seed every day by praying in tongues. Out of your inner being are flowing rivers of living water. That water is flooding your crop of seed and coming against the forces of darkness like a raging flood. And that flood is being driven by the Lord of the Breakthrough.

One last thought. Notice that David said, *"God hath broken in upon mine enemies* by mine hand." David's own hand was important to the breakthrough. He couldn't just sit by crying and say, "Please God, break through for me." God said, "Go up against the enemy." David had to go. So do you. Go up against the devil. You have the armor of God. Put it on and go.

You have your part. Do it. Keep doing it!

I want to be your prayer partner for a breakthrough in your life. I also want you to be standing with us for the breakthroughs we need in the ministry.

None of us at KCM can let up on any front. Preachers of the gospel in so many lands are being supported by this ministry. Believers are being taught who they are in Christ Jesus. Souls are being saved.

We'll never quit! We're going to break through with the help of your faith and intercession. Together, we'll open a hole in Satan's defense and the Lord of the Breakthrough will do the rest!

We love you with the *agape-hesed* (everlasting, merciful, all-encompassing, covenant love) of God which endures forever.

Your Brother in Christ,
Kenneth

November 1986

You've Been Given His Name

Dear Partner,

Did you know your name has been changed? Well it has. So has mine!

Intellectually, I've known it for a long time. Then a few weeks ago, the revelation hit my spirit more forcefully than ever before. It has profoundly affected my life. That's why I'm writing you about it today.

I want you to grasp, as I have, that your name is no longer the same as it was before you were born again. You've been brought into a covenant relationship through Jesus. You've been given His Name!

To fully appreciate what that means, you'll have to think about the blood covenant. Remember, when a person enters covenant with another, they become absolutely one with each other. They exchange coats saying, "All that I have and all that I am is now yours."

Actually when someone enters a covenant of blood, he is giving himself completely away. He is no longer his own. His assets and his debts, his strengths and his weaknesses belong forever to his covenant brother. In evidence of this, at the close of the covenant ceremony, the families involved exchange names with one another.

When you're in blood covenant with someone, that person's name becomes your name forever. You can't escape it—good or bad—it's yours.

When you accepted Jesus as your Lord and Savior, He took your name.

Your name was sin. Your name was weakness. Your name was whatever you inherited from Adam. Your life was ruled by fear, and hell was your home destination.

Then you decided to accept Jesus. He gave Himself away to you. You gave yourself away to Him. His life became yours. Your life became His. You turned loose of Adam as your father and received God as your Father.

You have become His heir—a joint heir with Jesus.

Ephesians 3:15 says the whole Body of Christ has been named after Him both in heaven and Earth. That includes you and me! Philippians 2:9 says He has been given a name that is above every name that is named.

You've been given that Name! Its authority is yours!

You can't call yourself discouraged anymore. That's not your name. You can't answer when the devil yells, "Hey, poor boy." That's not your name.

Jesus has taken those old names of yours. They're gone. Don't answer to them anymore.

When poverty calls, don't answer "Yes." Answer "No!" When your body calls itself sick, answer "No! That's not my name. I am healed." And when the devil tries to tell you you're alone and discouraged, answer him out loud, *"That's not in my covenant. I am strong in the Lord."*

Here's Who you are named after:-

Jesus	Prince of Peace
Mighty God	Wonderful Counselor
Wisdom	Lamb of God
Deliverer	Lord of Hosts
Lion of Judah	Root of David
Word of Life	Advocate
Author/Finisher of Our Faith	The Way
Provider	Healer
The Great I Am	Son of God
Helper	The Truth
Savior	Chief Cornerstone
King of Kings	Righteous Judge
Light of the World	Son of Righteousness
Chief Shepherd	Resurrection and Life
My Strength & Song	The Alpha and Omega

Now, don't just skim over that list. Stop and look at each of those names carefully. Then read them again out loud. Those are the names you've been given.

To anyone who knows about a covenant, a name is not just a handle. It's something to live up to. Can you live up to those names? Yes—because the power of God is in His name to bring that name to pass in your life.

The moment you accept God's names, the power to walk in them is yours. And, praise God, His names will cover any need you'll ever have! I want you to see this, not just in theory, but as a reality. You can put it to work in your life today!

First, briefly write down the single most urgent need you have right now. Then look over the list of God's names again and find the name that covers your need. Now write that name—*above your need!* Place it where you will see it daily and be reminded to speak it out loud.

Live as if that name you've chosen is the only name you have. For example, if you've been troubled by fear of some kind, don't cower around like your name is Fear. Stand up straight and roar at the devil like your name is the "Lion of Judah!"

It is, you know. Your name has been changed.

Meditate on the names of the Lord. They're your names now! And remember, no matter what the devil may try to bring against you, *"The name of the Lord is a strong tower: the righteous runneth into it, and is safe"* (Proverbs 18:10).

Until I write again, keep us in your prayers as you are in ours. You're always on my heart.

Your Brother in Christ Jesus,
Kenneth

December 1986

The Word—
From First to Last

Dear Partner,

I've spent a lot of time praying about this letter. And the Lord has given me something specific and urgent to say.

I believe as you read it, it's going to answer some questions you've been having. You're going to realize why some of your prayers have gone unanswered for so long. You're going to see why you've often felt like the victim of your circumstances, instead of a victor over them!

So I urge you to pray a few minutes right now, and then read the letter all the way through.

Not long ago, God brought a certain scripture to my attention. It is found in Revelation 1:8. Read it with me: *"I am Alpha and Omega, the beginning and the ending, saith the Lord, which is, and which was, and which is to come, the Almighty."*

That's Jesus speaking those words. I've always known they were significant, but recently I've realized more clearly than ever that through them Jesus is making a bold, exciting covenant statement. A statement that has a direct and life-changing impact on you, me and all the rest of His Covenant Partners.

Read it again. He is the beginning and the ending. He is Almighty!

I want you to realize, just as I did, that this is more than a general piece of information Jesus is giving about Himself. It's a thrilling and powerful truth you can apply now, today!

Think about it in terms of your own life. He started it. He'll finish it.

Your power is limited. You need someone mighty on your side. Well, He is Almighty! He is our God. Nothing was before Him. Nothing should be after Him. He is Jesus, Son of the Living God!

Now let me show you how to put this truth to work in practical, day-to-day living.

He is the beginning, right? So no matter what challenge or situation you may be facing right now, you need to start with Him. In John 1, the same man who recorded Jesus' words in Revelation tells us this: *Jesus is the Word.*

That means if you're going to start with Jesus, you're going to start with the Word. Don't do anything until you find out what the Word has to say about it. If Jesus is Almighty, then His Word is Almighty.

Colossians 3:17 says whatsoever you do in word or deed, do it all in the Name of the Lord Jesus. How can you do something in Jesus' Name without knowing what He has said about it? You can't! So go to the Word and find out!

Now, think about the situations you're facing in your life right now. You've probably given them plenty of thought already. You've prayed about them too. But have you taken the time to establish those thoughts and prayers on the Word of God?

If not, do it now!

I know you're busy. But let me tell you, you don't have anything to do that's more important than that. Your success is in and from the Word. Hebrews 1:3 tells us that Jesus is upholding all things by the Word of His power. How can you even hope to do anything successfully without it?

So start with the Word. Colossians 1:23 shows us what to do next. *"Continue in the faith grounded and settled, and be not moved away from the hope of the gospel, which ye have heard."* Let's take that scripture apart and follow it step by step.

Step 1: Continue in the faith.

The only way the devil can defeat you is to pressure you into throwing aside your stand of faith. Everything he does, every challenge he brings you is intended to make you doubt the Word of God. He's trying to get you to say, "Oh, my, it's not going to work for me this time." Don't let him do it!

Step 2: Be grounded and settled.

Be grounded firmly in the precious promises of God concerning your situation. Don't let go of the Word no matter what may happen. Settle it with God in prayer and stay with it forever.

Step 3: Be not moved away from the hope of the gospel which you have heard.

I don't care what anyone says. I don't care what someone may have written in a book. I don't care what someone said on television. I don't care what someone preached. If it's not in line with the Word, don't pay any attention to it. Don't be moved away from the gospel of the New Covenant. It's God's Word to you!

Start with the Word. Stay with the Word. End with the Word. Let His Word be the last word. Even my word or the word of your pastor is not the last word.

Make the Word of Jesus, your Covenant Brother and Lord, the Last Word!

You are now what the Word says you are. You can do what the Word says you can do. And you can have what the Word says you can have. Begin to believe that. Begin to say that out loud in faith.

> Jesus the Beginning.
> Jesus the Ending.
> Jesus the Everything.

Examine the situations about which you have been praying. Pick out the most urgent one. Have you established your prayers about it on the Word? If not, go to the Word and locate one or more of God's promises that assure you of victory over that situation.

Write them down. Pray them out loud. Pray the promises!

There's nothing—absolutely nothing—you can do about that situation that will have as much impact on it as applying the Word.

You don't have to wait and see the outcome to celebrate your victory. You have Jesus' Word on the matter, so you know beyond any doubt that your breakthrough is coming. Once you've settled the *alpha* Word, you *have* the *omega* Word.

Gloria and I and all of us here at Kenneth Copeland Ministries love you deeply.

> Your Brother in Victory,
> Kenneth

October 1989

No Deposit—No Return

Dear Partner,

Not long ago, a couple of my Partners were faced with a critical situation. It was a situation that would have made many people panic. But they used it as an opportunity to prove what the Word of God will do.

You see, when the crisis hit, these Partners were ready. They were prepared and established. They had planted the Word in their hearts so deeply that their first response was not one of fear, but of faith to stand on the Word.

Their whole story is thrilling. But what affected me most about it—and has continued to affect me ever since I heard it—was the phrase this young couple used when talking about the key to their victory. It is:

NO DEPOSIT—NO RETURN

That phrase means if you don't take the time to deposit the Word in your heart now, it won't be there in a crisis. There will be only doubt and unbelief where faith and power should be. Doubt and unbelief won't see you through.

In a situation like the one these Partners faced, that could be deadly. Here's what happened.

These Partners, Dr. Josh Prickett and his wife, Carin, were grocery shopping with their two children. Suddenly, 2-year-old Jonathan, who'd been sitting in the shopping cart, jumped to his feet, lost his balance and fell face first onto the store's concrete floor. His neck made a loud cracking sound as he hit. Even though Josh is a doctor, his initial response was not medical but spiritual. He immediately began to pray over his son in other tongues.

As they rushed Jonathan to the hospital, Carin held his limp body in her lap. He had no feeling in his arms and legs. He was unable to move and he seemed barely conscious. Yet she kept hearing the voice of the Lord rise up within her, saying, *My mercy hovers over your boy.*

When they reached the emergency room, X-rays were taken that revealed a serious skull fracture and a blockage in the airway of Jonathan's throat. Then the miraculous happened.

As a group from the Pricketts' local church began to pray, Jonathan—who had been lying pale and motionless on the hospital bed—sat straight up and said, "Daddy, I want a Dr. Pepper!" Then he hopped out of his bed and began playing on the floor of the emergency room as if nothing had ever happened.

Within the hour, when the final X-rays and CAT scans had been taken, neither the skull fracture nor the blockage could be found. They had completely disappeared!

Now let me show you something very important about this testimony.

The victory in this situation was not won when the damage to Jonathan's body disappeared. It was won all during the days, weeks and months prior to this incident when the Pricketts were listening to tapes, studying the Word, praying in the Spirit, meditating the Word and grounding themselves in the Word of healing and deliverance.

Because these Partners had spent time building a foundation on the Word, when this storm came, they were not devastated.

In fact, from the moment the storm hit, the situation was well under the direct authority and control of the Word. From the abundance of their hearts, the Pricketts spoke and declared the outcome from the beginning..."By Jesus' stripes, Jonathan is healed!"

Look at Luke 6:47-49:

[47]**Whosoever cometh to me, and heareth my sayings, and doeth them, I will show you to whom he is like:**

[48]**He is like a man which built an house, and digged deep, and laid the foundation on a rock: and when the flood arose, the stream beat vehemently upon that house, and could not shake it: for it was founded upon a rock.**

[49]**But he that heareth, and doeth not, is like a man that without a foundation built an house upon the earth; against which the stream did beat vehemently, and immediately it fell; and the ruin of that house was great.**

Now is the time for you to build a rock-solid foundation! Don't wait around until you need it. Start now. Start today. Don't let another minute go by without making a deep-rooted, uncompromising commitment to put the Word of God first place in your life. Remember...

NO DEPOSIT—NO RETURN

Galatians 6:7 says, *"Be not deceived; God is not mocked: for whatsoever a man soweth, that shall he also reap."*

Putting the Word first place and feeding on it daily must become the top priority in your life. Not just for a week or a month, but from now on. Day after day after day! That "daily-ness," that consistency, is so important. That's why the daily TV broadcasts we've been producing are so crucial. They're making the Word available to more and more people on a daily basis.

Here's another key to building your foundation: Don't try to fit the Word into your busy schedule. It won't work out. You'll find every excuse in the world to put off planting the Word into your heart.

Make your life fit around your time in the Word. Schedule it in first! Then, when you hit a spot where you really need it, the Word will be there working on your behalf. You won't even have to bring it up out of your spirit. It will just automatically flow out in power.

Eventually, nothing will be able to shake you.

You'll become a walking, talking manifestation of Psalm 112:7-8. You shall not be afraid of evil tidings: your heart will be fixed, trusting in the Lord. Your heart will be established [in the Word], and you shall not be afraid, until you see your desires upon your enemies!

I'm serious about this because this is serious business!

Gloria and I love you and appreciate you with all our hearts.

JESUS IS LORD!
Kenneth

February 1987

Take Your Stand...Now!

Dear Partner,

May grace and spiritual peace be yours from God our Father, and the Lord Jesus Christ, Whose we are and Whom we serve.

This letter to you is one of encouragement and strength...strength to do what you know you should do...inner strength from the Holy Spirit to do what you must do in order to rise to the place where God wants you to be.

Where does God want you to be? In victory!

He wants you to be in victory in His Name—victory in your spirit, victory in your soul, your thought life and the things of your will, and victory in your emotions. He died so you could have victory over your physical body in every area, including deliverance from sickness, disease, bondage and bad habits.

God wants you to live in victory in every area of your life! Always!

Let's look at what the Bible says in Ephesians 6:10-11. Read it very carefully: *"Finally,* [this is final, we *must* do this] *my brethren, be strong in the Lord, and in the power of his might.* [Not your might—His might. Now notice the next verse.] *Put on the whole armour of God, that you may be able to stand against the wiles of the devil."*

If you're going to be victorious, you must understand that you cannot stand against Satan's works without the full armor of God. But once you put on the full armor of God and His strength, you can stand against anything Satan has!

Not only have I read that truth in the Scriptures, but I've seen it in action. My own mother was a living example of it.

I remember a time some years before she went to be with the Lord that she began having terrible pains in her chest. She prayed, but the pain only grew worse. She increased her praying and took her stand on the Word, yet her health continued to go downhill. Gloria and I laid hands on her and joined in faith with her and Dad.

Day after day, she continued to fight that illness—not in her own strength, but in the armor and might of God. Here's how she did it:

First, she reminded the devil that she was a child of God. (She put on the helmet of salvation.)

Second, she told him she had certain rights in God's kingdom. (That's her breastplate of righteousness.)

She quoted the Word to him. (She went after him with the sword of the Spirit.) She also quoted it to herself (girding her loins with the truth) night and day.

And she never stopped going. (She kept her feet shod with the gospel.) She kept going to places and meetings where the Word was preached in power. She kept placing herself in the presence of anointed men and women of God even though it was extremely difficult to do and very, very uncomfortable.

Sometimes her lungs would fill with fluid. Sometimes she would lose her balance and look like a drunk person because of the vertigo. Her head hurt. It would spin in dizziness and make her sick.

Still, she prayed, praised and kept her stand.

She had every opportunity to give up and die. It would have been so easy for her just to say, "I'm over 70 years of age, I've lived for God all these years and I've had a good life. My body hurts so badly, I think I'll just quit and go on home to be with the Lord." The temptation to do that was there constantly.

Instead, she declared her faith. She continued to say with her mouth that she was healed by the stripes of Jesus. She continued to pray in other tongues in the Spirit, not only for herself but for others. She stayed with her ministry of intercessory prayer (Ephesians 6:18).

It took months, then years, but one day she woke up in the morning feeling refreshed and, as she put it, "Brand new!" She was physically strong. All symptoms were gone, and everything was working normally. Praise God!

It took every piece of armor, but the Word worked!

She wasn't willing to take that armor off, regardless of how she felt. She knew that she had to keep standing in faith, fully armed with God's power to successfully defeat the enemy.

The point I want you to understand here is this: When you take your stand in the might of the Lord, you get stronger. And the longer you stand—the stronger you get! You don't get weaker as time goes by, you get stronger!

So stay in His might. Stay in His Word. Don't talk the problem, talk the answer.

Romans 11:20 says we stand by faith. Faith comes by

hearing and hearing by the Word. Don't lie down and take a break from the Word just because your body hurts or because you don't feel like reading the Word for some reason or the other. You can't draw on God's strength when you're spending your time on things that don't minister God's strength to you.

Stand—having done all!

You can do it. You have everything it takes to face the challenge you're up against right now.

Dress yourself for battle. Put on the full armor of God. You may feel silly, but that's OK—do it anyway! Start with the helmet of salvation and get dressed.

Give. Giving opens the floodgates of heaven. Giving puts you in a receiving position. It prepares you to receive. You want *God's* best so you do *your* best.

Go to where the power of God is. Get to a church where they pray and preach the Word. Listen to tapes of powerful, faith-filled messages continually, night and day. Read your Bible every morning, at every meal and before bed.

Walk in love with everyone. If you slip, repent immediately and stay in love.

You can do it! If you didn't have what it takes to make it in this dangerous generation, God would have caused you to be born in some other era.

Take your stand now—and remember, all of us here at KCM are standing with you. We love you and pray for you every day.

Your Friend and Partner,
Kenneth

May 1987

God Wants You Well!

Dear Partner,

Some time ago I was in the mighty Rocky Mountains of Colorado enjoying the majesty of those grand snowcapped peaks and marveling over God's works of faith, and I began to pray for my Partners.

Suddenly, a message from the Lord shot through my spirit, clear and strong. It was this:

God Wants You Well!

He wants you healthy and strong in every single area of your life. He wants you to be spiritually strong. Strong in faith. Strong in the Word. Strong in redemption. Strong in the love of God.

He wants you to be well in your mind, to be strong and stable emotionally. He wants you to have a healthy will, a will that's aligned with His will. He wants your body to be well. He wants you free from the bondages of pain, sickness and cares, free from the worries and woes of this earthly life.

Your heavenly Father wants you well! It's hard for me to find words that express that as powerfully as the Lord expressed it to me. In fact, I got so excited about it that I immediately wanted to be a part of getting that message to God's people.

"Lord, what do You want me to do?" I asked.

His answer to my question was clear. God has commissioned us—you, Gloria and me—to help teach the Body of Christ the day-by-day principles of living a life of victory in Jesus. And He's commissioning us to get it done faster and more effectively than ever before!

There's no more time for the Body of Christ to limp along, uninformed and unprepared for the devil's attacks.

In fact, here's what the Lord told me. He said, *The further you go, the more dangerous things on the Earth will become. People will have to grow in the realities of redemption and the 'how tos' of living by faith in order to live in the great overcoming way that I have planned for them.*

Today, through this letter, I want to stimulate that growth in you. I want you to realize that God wants you (yes, *you!*) well. How can you get excited about teaching others about victory and healing until you're experiencing victory and health yourself?

You can't!

So the new work God has given us to do begins right here. With you. With your family.

Today I want you to catch the vision of Jesus, arms outstretched, smiling (as we say) from ear to ear, saying, *Tell them I want them well.*

He gave Himself in death so that we could be well. He was raised in life and is ever making intercession for us *now* so that we can be well. He wants us to be healthy and strong as a witness to a world that's filled with terror—a witness of His love, His grace and His power.

What a thrilling time this is to be alive!

In the days to come, you and I are going to become so established in God's Word and power that nothing in the world order will be able to phase us. Just like the man in Psalm 112:7, we shall not be afraid of evil tidings because our hearts will be fixed, trusting in the Lord.

Praise God!

Your Brother in Christ Jesus,
Kenneth Copeland

April 1987

Draw the Faith Line

Dear Partner,

I really believe your prayers for me have helped me win a major victory in my life. Let me tell you the exciting story behind this victory.

Several years ago in one of our Believers' Conventions, I hurt my voice during a song one night. I felt something pull and break deep in my throat. I felt as though a hot knife had cut through it. By the end of the service, I was in real pain.

I reminded the Lord that some years before, I had placed the care of my voice in His hands. Then, I began to stand in faith for my healing. Most of the pain left that night and the rest was gone in a few days, but one problem remained. My singing voice just wouldn't work right.

The devil tried to tell me I would never sing again, and even if I did, it would never be the same.

But he's a liar—and this story proves it!

Jesus not only healed me, He sent me a voice coach and teacher who trained me and strengthened my voice beyond anything I ever knew was available. As a result, I recorded an album called *Great Songs of Praise*.

But I'm no lone ranger. I wasn't standing in faith, believing God for that healing all by myself. There were people standing with me. Praying with me. Joining their faith with mine. Friends and Partners like you. Even though I didn't announce it publicly, as you prayed for Gloria and me and for this ministry in the Spirit, God used your prayers to bring me to that place of victory, and I'm grateful to you.

In return for your love and partnership, I want to share something with you today that's extremely valuable. It's something I've learned that can help you receive from God when you face times of great need like the one I just described.

It's something I call stepping over the faith line.

A faith line is what you need when you want God to do the "impossible" in your life. It's what you need when you want to be firm in your faith and yet you keep wavering back and forth between your circumstances and God's promises—trusting first in one, then in the other.

Just think about Abraham for a moment. You know, God made some promises to him that must have sounded pretty wild under the circumstances. Abraham had the same set of natural facts to deal with that we do. He knew there was no natural way for God's promises to him to come true.

Yet in Romans 4:19-20, the Word says *Abraham gave glory to God, being strong in faith*. It also says he considered not his own body. In other words, Abraham ignored the natural evidence around him and believed only God's promise.

Somewhere he stepped across the line of faith.

He made an irreversible decision to go with the Word of God. He made a final commitment. He chose to step past the point of no return. And if you and I are ever going to see God do the impossible in our lives, we're going to have to do the same thing!

How do you draw the faith line?

You have to begin with the Word. Faith cometh by hearing and hearing by the Word of God. You simply can't draw the faith line without knowing and believing what God's Word has promised you about your situation.

So search the promises of God and purposely believe what He has said, and is saying, about your need. Meditate on those promises until faith rises in your heart.

Then draw the line of faith.

When I'm ready to draw the line of faith, I draw it in my mind. I draw it in my heart. Many times, I literally draw it across the floor in my prayer room. Then in Jesus' Name, I step across it.

From that moment on, I speak only as if that miracle has already taken place. I act as if God has already done it. From that moment on, I call things that be not as if they already were.

There's no turning back!

I turn my back on the problems, on the doubts, on the unbeliefs, and turn my face toward Jesus. Then I keep the Word constantly before my eyes and on my lips. As Hebrews 3:1 says, I consider Jesus my Apostle and High Priest of my confession.

Are you ready to step over that faith line concerning some need in your life? If so, here's what I want you to do.

1. Find the scriptural promises that cover that need.

2. Meditate on them night and day until faith rises up in your heart. (Don't ever try to take this next step without first taking steps one and two!)

3. Finally, draw a line and say out loud: "In the presence of God, Jesus and the Holy Spirit, in the presence of all the angels in this room and in the devil's face, I am stepping across the line of faith. From this day forward, I give God the praise and the glory in the Name of Jesus."

Let's step across the faith line together! We can do it. More than that—we must do it. God's time has come. Until I hear from you, I remain—

Yours in the Service of Jesus Christ Our Lord,
Kenneth Copeland

August 1987

Give Your Way to Victory

Dear Partner,

We are standing with you against the forces of darkness and lack the same way we are standing against them here at KCM. We are daily making intercession for you in prayer. I am believing you are doing the same for us.

You and I together are taking the Word of Faith to the Body of Christ all over the Earth. You are so very important to us and such an important part of what we are doing in the kingdom of God.

I am not doing the work of this ministry alone. We are doing it together!

You are working with me—and Satan is trying to stop you just as he's trying to stop me. That's why I feel such an urgency about interceding for you right now. This is a powerful time. A time for giving.

Remember, God always relies on giving. He depends on the power in the law of increase to overcome attacks against Him. For God so loved the world He gave. He gave his best—Jesus! His *only* Son! And He gained *many* sons in return.

Seed-plant and harvest is God's plan for success. It's His way. Gloria and I have made it our way. It's KCM's way. It's the way of Life. Let's look at 2 Corinthians 9:8, 10:

"And God is able to make all grace abound toward you; that ye, always having all sufficiency in all things, may abound to every good work. Now he that ministereth seed to the sower both minister bread for your food, and multiply your seed sown, and increase the fruits of your righteousness."

Read those verses again very carefully, noticing that God wants you *always having sufficiency.*

Grace has abounded toward you for that reason. Grace comes from heaven, so it's not bound to lack, sickness, disease, fear or anything else of the world order.

Now look again at verse 10: "He [God] that ministereth seed to the sower both minister bread for your food, and multiplies your seed sown, and increases the fruits of your [righteousness] right-standing with God."

God increases the fruits of your righteousness! What do those fruits include? Health, prosperity, peace of mind and abundance in every area of life—spirit, soul and body. That's the reason Jesus said seek first the kingdom and His right-standing and *all* these things will be added unto you.

God has given you seed. Look for it. There are all kinds of things you can give. Start with giving a smile and go from there. Don't let things pile up around you—give, give, give, give.

Expect your daily bread to come. Pray for it daily. I receive my daily bread by faith according to 2 Corinthians 9:10. I also receive my seed sown multiplied so that I can be sufficient and give more.

You can do the same! Look to God for the fruits of your righteousness to be increased. You became the righteousness of God when you made Jesus the Lord of your life. His blood placed you in right-standing with God giving you all that's His. Through Jesus, all that the Father has is yours.

Healing is yours!

Deliverance is yours!

Joy is yours!

Faith is yours!

The love of God is yours!

The Name of Jesus is yours...and on and on down the line!

Believe right now for the fruits of righteousness to be increased in your life as you give.

You should be in a constant state of thanksgiving for the increase of your harvest. (See 2 Corinthians 9:11.) Develop a giving attitude which is also a winning attitude. Be like David in Psalm 35:27. Shout for joy and be glad and continually say, *"Let the Lord be magnified, which hath pleasure in the prosperity of his servant!"*

Do it all day long!

Malachi 3:11 says God has rebuked the devourer for our sakes. God does not rebuke Satan over and over again. He doesn't have to—He has done His part. Satan *is* rebuked!

Show that scripture to the devil and remind him he has been rebuked and that you're standing on God's Word for it. Tell him to get his hands off your finances *now!* Remind him you are not bound to the world order but that you are all sufficient in all things including the increasing of all the fruits of your righteousness.

If it's healing you need, give and expect that fruit to be increased. It already belongs to you in Christ Jesus. Whatever it is that you need, give and expect God's best with all your heart.

Finally, don't wait until you can see the increase. Start acting and talking as if it was already in your hand where you can see it.

Stay with it. Be like Jesus. Don't change. Stay on the Word in love and faith until they say about you what is said of Him—you're the same yesterday, today and forever.

As you give, shout for joy and be glad, for together we shall see the salvation and the glory of the Lord.

Love,
Kenneth

September 1990

No Prize for Compromise

Dear Partner,

Years ago, I was in an Oral Roberts evangelistic meeting where I heard him make a statement that was to change my life forever. He said, "What you compromise to keep, you will lose."

Those words burned into my spirit and branded my brain. They rang in my ears. For days afterward that phrase was all I could think about.

Some time later, I heard Kenneth Hagin say, "Once you've taken a stand on God's Word, if you're willing to stand forever, you won't have to stand very long."

When Gloria and I entered this ministry, we made lifelong, forever-settled commitments before God. We made up our minds and settled forever certain things about our calling, certain things about our financial lives, certain things about our family. We settled forever between us that we would not compromise God's Word. We determined that God's Word is true and it works whether it looks like it or not.

From that day to this, Gloria and I have never prayed about those commitments again. They are settled. We never allow ourselves to question whether or not God's Word will produce overcoming victory in our lives. If something is wrong, the failure is with us, not with God or His Word. That is settled!

That kind of unquestioning confidence is the most basic rule you must keep if you're going to successfully run the race of faith.

Rule? Yes, rule! There are rules to this life of faith. As 2 Timothy 2:5 says, *"If a man also strive for masteries, yet is he not crowned, except he strive lawfully."*

If someone in a race is running for the prize, there is no prize unless he keeps the rules. Is it all right for someone to cheat just because they're running last? No. There are a lot of people who think so, but that still doesn't make it right.

We, as believers, must run this race according to the rules of faith, not according to the selfish, honorless rules we are surrounded by in this world.

Have you ever heard the phrase, "I believe that person is basically honest"? What does that mean? How could a person be basically honest? One is either honest or he's not. What that phrase really means is, "that person doesn't lie unless he's put under pressure." That kind of compromise-under-pressure attitude is not good enough for people of faith.

Look at the third and fourth verses of that same chapter in Timothy: *"Thou therefore endure hardness, as a good soldier of Jesus Christ. No man that warreth entangleth himself with the affairs of this life; that he may please him who hath chosen him to be a soldier."*

Every one of us is going to encounter "hardness" in this life. But we're to endure the hard places as an honorable, well-trained soldier endures the hardships of training and mortal combat without deserting his comrades and running away.

How can you develop that kind of endurance? By deciding here and now that you are *never* going to compromise. No one can face mortal enemy fire without turning to run unless somewhere, sometime in his life he has made a deep inner decision not to compromise—even if it means his own death. That's true in spiritual battle as well.

"Yeah, but Brother Copeland, if I hadn't done what I did, I might have lost my car...I might have lost my job."

"Well, you know how it is, brother. The people won't give unless you really let them know how bad things are."

Remember, what you compromise to keep you will lose! Sometime, someplace, the stand must be made. Your victory declaration must be made.

The Word says I'm healed. So I say, "I'm healed! I'll never change. That's it. No matter what it looks like, even if I die, I'll go to heaven shouting, 'By His stripes I'm healed.'"

That's the kind of uncompromising stand you and I must establish in our lives in order to carry out this end-time calling that's on us as individuals and also on the Body of Christ.

Jesus did not compromise in the Garden of Gethsemane, and He's not seated on the throne of compromise. There is no compromise in His Word. It's settled forever both in heaven and on the Earth and will never pass away.

There is no compromise in His Name. It is exalted forever above every name—*every name!*

Cancer? His Name is above it. Poverty? His Name is above it. Fear? His Name is above it and has authority over it.

Let the devil do the compromising. If you don't compromise, he'll have to!

I believe this letter will encourage you to settle and establish your heart forever in God's Word. Put it first place. Make it final authority in your life. It will never leave you nor forsake you.

Gloria and I are standing with you. All the KCM staff send their love and prayers.

Love,
Kenneth

P.S. Read Psalm 112 very carefully. It's the picture of the kind of life the uncompromised Word will produce. Hallelujah!

September 1987

Your Victory Is Up Ahead

Dear Partner,

Thank God that in Jesus we are a people of victory! His blood has declared our victory in Him! His Word makes us free!

As I sit here writing this letter, I realize that you may have been under a lot of pressure lately. You may look at the circumstances around you and be tempted to say, "Brother Copeland, God's Word hasn't made me free."

But don't do that.

We're not through yet! You are free and your victory is up ahead.

Take a careful look at Philippians 3:13-14: *"Brethren, I do not count myself to have apprehended; but one thing I do, forgetting those things which are behind and reaching forward to those things which are ahead, I press toward the goal for the prize of the upward call of God in Christ Jesus" (New King James Version).*

The first thing this verse tells us to do is to forget those things which are behind. There are three ways you can do that.

First—Get your mind off the past.

You can't go forward when you're holding on to the past. We can't have the speed and force we need to press back the forces of darkness as long as we're looking over our shoulders. Fear looks back! Faith looks forward! Jesus is always up ahead. Heaven is in front of us. The biggest, most rewarding job is still ahead for you and me. We can't afford to let Satan's interference stop us now.

Here's the second way to forget those things which are behind:

Don't dwell on yesterday's miracles.
Thank God for them, but we're moving forward to even greater outpourings of God's glory. It will take all of us going forward together, holding forth the Word of God in faith, prayer and love, to do our part in what the Spirit is bringing to pass—just *up ahead!*

Third (this is somewhat of a play on words, but the principle is important):

Forget those things which are behind—literally!
Maybe you're behind on your bills. Or maybe you feel like you're behind in your health or your commitment to God or your prayer life. Don't dwell on the ways in which you are behind! All have sinned and fallen short in different areas of their lives. God knows that. Repent and go forward! God isn't holding anything against you. He's made provision for your shortcomings and failures.

Begin to pray every day, *"Thy kingdom come, Thy will be done! in my life today. The Lord is my Shepherd, I do not want."* Stop working hard to "get" back into God's will. Let Him lead you into it.

Relax! Stop looking back at the past. It's over. Everything God has for you is *up ahead*. Let's go for it in faith and joy.

Please understand, all this doesn't mean you become irresponsible where your bills and other responsibilities are concerned. It simply means that by going forward in faith, you will open the door for the Holy Spirit to show you how to receive from Him everything you need to straighten out all your problems and failures—whatever they are.

Now, in closing, look again at verse 14. There the Apostle Paul says, "*I* press *toward the goal....*"

What does that mean?

To press means to put under pressure. Pressure. That's what Satan has been doing to you. He's been applying pressure to your mind, your body, your finances, and every other part in your life he can get his hands on.

Now the time has come to turn the tables and put pressure on him!

You can put pressure on the kingdom of darkness by praying in the spirit and standing on God's Word in faith. Stand! Praise! Shout! Confess the Word of God!

That will bring a mighty pressure to bear against the devil's kingdom. The force of it will be greater than you can even imagine.

Press into God. Draw close to Him. Luke 16:16 says we press into the kingdom of God. Mark 3:10 says people pressed, or rushed, upon Jesus. Rush to Him in prayer. Rush to Him in His Word.

Press into God by "adding to." Add a few minutes more to your prayer time. Praise a few minutes more. Stretch yourself. Press through the limitations your flesh has tried to impose on you.

You don't have to impress God. He loves you already. You just need to grow so you can receive more and know more of Him. He loves you so!

Sit down right now and pray and meditate on these things. See yourself turning from the past toward the future God has for us in Jesus. Settle in your spirit and in your mind what your most important goals are—the goals that are up ahead for you.

Now, see yourself rising up and marching toward those marks with faith in your heart as the Holy Spirit leads you and gives you His strength to get there.

We are marching, serving God, together.

Because you and my other Partners and friends listened to the Holy Spirit where this ministry is concerned, the financial pressure the devil put on us has been broken. Praise God, that attack is behind us now. Rejoice with us. We are going forward in power.

All of us here at KCM are experiencing the love of Jesus more than ever in our history, and it's flowing through us to you.

Thank you for your prayers. I feel them.

Love,
Kenneth

P.S. Don't put off praying and meditating over the things in this letter. Do it now or at least before the day is over. Go forward!

October 1987

"Tell Them How Much I Love Them"

Dear Partner,

I hope I can convey to you through this letter what I heard one day as I was praying for you and all my other Partners. Maybe you should pray for a moment before you read the rest of it. I want its message to come through to you with the same impact it has had on me.

A few days ago, I was walking through a park praying and I just asked the Lord a simple question, *"What do you want me to tell my Partners in my next letter?"* Without a moment's hesitation, the answer came ringing through my spirit and my mind.

Tell them how much I love them.

It was so filled with love and compassion that it defies words to express it. The rest of the day, all that night and throughout the next day, all I could think of was 1 John 4:16: *"And we have known and believed the love that God hath to us."* Another translation says, "...believed the love God has *in* us."

We've all read about God's love. We've heard it. But I don't think we really believe it.

If we really believed the love He has for us, it would totally change everything about us and everything around us.

Jesus said for us to love one another even as He loves us. What a change it makes when I get a revelation of just how much He loves me. After all, that's how much He loves *you*.

Let's take a new look at Hebrews 4:15-16: *"For we have not an high priest which cannot be touched with the feeling of our infirmities; but was in all points tempted like as we are, yet without sin. Let us therefore come boldly unto the throne of grace, that we may obtain mercy, and find grace to help in time of need."*

Jesus has been through everything we've been through. And He understands it all so well that as our High Priest He is saying, "Don't be shy about it. I've been there. Come boldly to the throne of grace that you may obtain mercy and find grace to help in time of need."

God is in love! He is so in love, that He has given everything He has. He has given it to you now through His grace (which is more than enough). Second Corinthians 9:8 says that grace brings *all* sufficiency in *all things* and that God is able to make all grace *abound* toward you.

Does that mean His grace is more than enough if someone has some horrible disease like AIDS? Yes!

"But what about my terrible past?"

That's what mercy is for. *Obtain it!* God is in love, and His mercy and grace are more than enough.

"But how do I get Him to use that grace to heal my body and supply my needs?"

That's the beauty of it all, He's already done it. All we have to do is receive it.

Believe the love He has for us. It has already been released in the blood of Jesus.

Believe the love. It has already been released in Jesus' Name.

Believe the love. It has already been released in His Word.

Believe the love. Grace has already defeated cancer. Grace has already defeated AIDS. Grace has already defeated the curse. It has no power left over those who believe the love.

What a shame for someone to suffer and die some horrible death at the hands of a sickness or disease that's already been defeated—especially when it's just because of not believing the love He has for us. He is love!

Meditate 1 John 4:16 over and over. Say it to yourself again and again all day: "I believe the love Jesus has for me." Let it get down in your heart.

Eventually the boldness will arise inside you to go to the throne and receive the sufficiency, the grace, to overcome the things the forces of darkness have brought into your life.

Take time to pray about your most important need. Then write it down. Look at it, and say out loud, "I believe the love Jesus has for me!"

Gloria and I believe the love Jesus has for you. We stand with you.

We pray that the Holy Spirit will use this letter to gloriously enlarge your revelation of Jesus' love toward you.

We love you more every day we pray for you, and we pray for you every day.

Your Covenant Partner and Friend,
Kenneth

November 1987

Jesus and His Word Are One

Dear Partner,

My, how God loves you and me! When it comes time to write this letter to you each month, I begin to sense the weight of His love in me, urging me to get His Word to you to help build your faith and trust in Jesus.

I want to share with you today about pressing into a closer and more intimate relationship with your heavenly Father. James 4:8 says, *"Draw nigh to God, and he will draw nigh to you."* That's a promise!

Your number one step in drawing closer to God is to realize that you know God first in His Word. That's just the opposite of what most people try to do. They try to know Him first in their feelings and that just won't work.

Time spent meditating in the New Testament is time spent with Jesus. Letting the Word dominate your thinking is allowing the Holy Spirit to have control over your mind.

Too many Christians are mentally dominated by fear. The Scripture says, *"We've not been given a spirit of fear, but of power, love, and of a sound mind."* A sound mind is one thing, a fear-filled mind is another. If you'll let the Word dominate your thoughts, it will bring your mind to a place of soundness.

Constant feeding on God's Word and acting on it causes the Word to dwell in us richly (Colossians 3:16). Then it will begin to bear prayer fruit. Jesus Himself said that it would! In John 15:7, He said, *"If ye abide in me, and my words abide in you, ye shall ask what ye will, and it shall be done unto you."* That's a glorious promise.

When His Word is dwelling in you richly, then Jesus is dwelling in you richly. Acting on the Word brings Jesus on the scene of action! Jesus and His Word are one!

Things in this old world aren't getting any better. I keep hearing the Holy Spirit saying, "Press in. If you don't, you won't make it. If you do, you will see more glorious outpourings than you can imagine."

Those who don't make time for the Word and for prayer are going from disaster to disaster. But those who do make time for the Word, prayer and faith are going to defeat the disasters and turn them into glory, in Jesus' Name.

I believe you are one of those people who are headed for glory. So, stand up! Look your situation right in the eye and shout God's living Word into its face! That Word is alive! It's sharper than any two-edged sword! Don't give up. Don't turn it loose. Don't get discouraged. It's working out there in the spirit realm where it counts.

Let's look at what we've learned:

1. **Draw closer to Jesus. Press into Him.**

2. **Get to know Him in His Word.**

3. Time spent meditating in the New Testament is time spent with Jesus. Spend time in the Word!

4. Allow the Holy Spirit to have control over your mind by letting the Word dominate your thinking.

5. Constant feeding on God's Word will cause the Word to dwell in you richly. Feed on the Word!

6. Acting on the Word brings Jesus on the scene. Act on the Word!

7. Don't get discouraged. The Word of God is working out there in the spirit realm where it counts.

You can't afford to be moved by what you feel. What are your feelings worth? Are they worth your not receiving from God? No! Are they worth your faith not working? Absolutely not!

Rise up in the living Word, and it will rise up in you and bring you to the victory that you need in Jesus. Praise God!

You'll be in heaven before you really understand how important you are to this ministry and to Gloria and me. We love you and pray for you every day.

In Covenant Love,
Kenneth

January 1988

Be Consistently Constant

Dear Partner,

With every day that goes by, the deep comforting of the Holy Spirit that comes from your prayers and support grows more powerful inside me. Thank you from the bottom of my heart.

The Lord has been impressing me to share a Bible truth with you that is almost unheard of in the Body of Christ today. It's one of the most powerful and practical things the Bible teaches. It's based on a simple but profound truth in Hebrews 13:8: *Jesus is the same yesterday, today and forever.*

Now, let's dig into the truth of that statement. Jesus is always the same. That means He is consistently constant. Now, put that fact together with what He said in Mark 4:30. There, Jesus compared the kingdom of God to seed being planted and growing. How does the seed grow? All at once?

No. It is consistently constant. It grows constantly— 24 hours a day—a little all the time until it accomplishes what it was created to do.

Most people don't operate that way spiritually. They study and pray really hard for a few days, then quit until some disaster comes. Then they make a mad attempt to pray and stand on the Word—all the while realizing that for some strange reason, they are just not strong enough to walk in the miraculous realm the way they should.

James 1:4 says, *"Let patience have her perfect work, that ye may be perfect and entire, wanting nothing."*

The word translated patience means "constancy." You have need of consistent constancy. Let it (patience or constancy) do its work that you may be completely without need or want!

Jesus said in Luke 21:19, *"In your patience [being constant] possess ye your souls."* In almost every scripture in the New Testament, patience, or constancy, is coupled with faith. Look at these examples:

- Second Thessalonians 1:4 says patience and faith account for endurance in persecutions and tribulations.
- In 1 Timothy 6:11-12, we are told to follow after, or develop, faith and patience in order to fight the good fight of faith.
- In Titus 2:2, we are told to be sound, or solid, in faith, love and constancy.
- In James 5:10, patience is given credit for the endurance of prophets.
- In 2 Peter 1:6, patience is listed as one of the spiritual elements that must be added to our faith to keep us from being barren or unfruitful. This thing is powerful!
- In Hebrews 12:1, we are instructed to run the race of faith with consistent constancy.

Patience! The power twin of faith!

What makes Jesus the same always? What makes Jesus so

constant? The Word! He always keeps the Word which is settled forever in heaven.

When we begin to truly be doers of the Word and not just hearers only, we then begin to know what all this means. We begin to act as though the New Testament is true every hour of every day regardless of what comes or how we feel. We begin to be constant.

When people speak well of me, I stay on the Word. It's my strength and favor.

When people speak ill of me, I stay on the Word. It's why I act the way I do. It's my strength and will see me through persecutions.

So really, it doesn't matter what people say. What matters is what the Word says. It is forever. It is what counts. It says I'm healed whether sickness tries to come on me or not. It says my needs are met in Christ Jesus whether circumstances look like it or not.

Now here again constancy becomes important.

In order to constantly act as though the Word of God is done in my life, I must be consistent and constant in keeping the Word before my eyes, in my ears and in the midst of my heart—not just when I want to or when I feel like it, but constantly. Like the seed, I must grow in the Word a little all the time.

Every day a line here, a line there, a tape here, a tape there.

Read letters like this every day. If you don't have time, make time. Put God's Word first in your life.

Run the race looking unto Jesus—constantly, consistently, faithfully—and you will emerge victoriously without wants or needs. Most importantly, you will be able to minister to those who are hurting like you and I were hurting before we became consistently constant on the Word of God, looking at Jesus every moment of our lives.

Study this and act on it. The strength of your faith will astound and thrill you.

I really need your prayers right now. Pray Ephesians 6:19-20: *"And for me, that utterance may be given unto me, that I may open my mouth boldly, to make known the mystery of the gospel, For which I am an ambassador in bonds: that therein I may speak boldly, as I ought to speak."*

My bones are afire with the desire to get more of God's Word out to meet the needs of the people.

Help me pray the hindrances out of our way such as money, equipment, future planning in the expansion of television, planning of future meetings, being at the right place at the right time in the Holy Spirit.

Sometimes it looks so big I think, *Who, me?*

But then I realize, *No, not just me, but* all of us together.

Together in faith, in Jesus, we can get it done! Better than that—we *will* get it done!

I love you in Jesus,
Ken

March 1988

Say It—Say It—Say It Believe It!

Dear Partner,

"Whosoever shall say unto this mountain, Be thou removed, and be thou cast into the sea; and shall not doubt in his heart, but shall believe that those things which he saith shall come to pass; he shall have whatsoever he saith" (Mark 11:23).

A number of years ago, I heard Brother Kenneth Hagin make the following statement after reading Mark 11:23, *"That verse says 'say it' three times and 'believe it' once. If we want to receive something from God, we have to say it three times as much as we believe it."*

That really took root in me and I have proven in my own life that it is absolutely true.

Even those, or should I say, *especially* those who know better have let this vital Bible truth slip in their daily lives.

Jesus said in Luke 6:45 and Mark 11:23 that we have what we say. Look around you. Whatever you have is a product of what you've been saying. In order to change what you have, you must change what you're saying.

Recently I was praying for someone and I heard the Holy Spirit say, *Words are process starters.*

Healing is a process. Prosperity is a process. These

spiritual processes work when they are put to work by faith. They continue until the promise of God is obtained— if they are not interrupted by an enemy process such as unbelief.

Words start the process. James 3:3-4 says, *"Behold, we put bits in the horses' mouths, that they may obey us; and we turn about their whole body. Behold also the ships, which though they be so great, and are driven of fierce winds, yet are they turned about with a very small helm, whithersoever the governor listeth."*

Notice here that James is pointing out that the course, or destination, of both the horse and the ship is controlled by the captain. Then in verse 5 he says, *"Even so the tongue..."*

You are the captain James is talking about. The tongue is the rudder in *your* hand. It is *your* responsibility to fill your mouth with God's Words thereby giving Him control of your life.

Notice also from verse 5 that the tongue is the kindling that sets on fire *the course of nature.* Somewhere down the line, your tongue, or your words, started the process of whatever you now have in your life.

Let's look at the words of Jesus in Mark 4:26-27: *"So is the kingdom of God, as if a man should cast seed into the ground; And should sleep, and rise night and day, and the seed should spring and grow up, he knoweth not how."*

Jesus said the whole kingdom of God operates under the spiritual law of seed-plant and harvest. Man lives under the law of gradual spiritual growth. The words of your mouth are the seeds that determine whether or not what you have is from heaven or hell.

Now, look at James 3:6. It says the tongue *"is set on fire of hell."* Hell knows it cannot do anything with your life if it can't get hold of your tongue. However, the devil also knows if he can capture your tongue, he can do very nearly anything he wants to with you even though legally he's not your lord.

I have learned that he is most successful with seemingly unimportant words and sayings that become habits. Such words are habitually spoken daily over and over until they are built into our consciousness so deeply that even when the harvest of sickness, financial disaster or whatever bad situation comes, we don't realize that it was connected to those simple but deadly words.

Those words set in motion the course of natural things. Proverbs 18:7 says that a fool's mouth is his destruction and his lips (or words) snare his soul.

Now let's look at this law of gradual spiritual growth from another angle—faith in God!

When Jesus' disciples asked Him to increase their faith, He answered by reminding them of this seed-plant-harvest law. If you want your faith to increase, plant it. It will grow. How do you plant it? By saying words.

"And the apostles said unto the Lord, Increase our faith. And the Lord said, If ye had faith as a grain of mustard seed, ye might say unto this sycamine tree, Be thou plucked up by the root, and be thou planted in the sea; and it should obey you" (Luke 17:5-6).

Faith must be planted, or started, with words, then allowed to grow. Everything in the kingdom of God is under this law. Love, joy, peace, even salvation or the new birth began when confession was made unto it.

I believe it's very obvious now what must be done. We must change course. We must head our lives in a different direction—from death to life, sickness to health, failure to success. To do that, we must change what we've been saying. That's a lot easier said than done.

But that's the key—*it must be said* in order to be done.

How do you change what you've been saying?

First, realize that it can't be done with natural, human strength. This is a spiritual law, so it must be carried out with spiritual power. James 3:7-8 says the tongue can't be tamed with the same power with which man tames animals. He goes on to point out that it takes God's wisdom from above. Jesus said God's Word is His wisdom. He also said His words are spirit and they are life. In other words, it takes God's words to tame our tongues.

Second, you must repent before God for ever allowing your tongue to be used by anyone except the Holy Spirit. Then give Jesus your tongue. Be determined to speak His words of love, faith, joy, peace and grace. Words of faith stop the fiery darts of hell.

Third, do what Jesus said to do in Mark 4:24. Take heed, or listen, to what you hear. What you continually listen to, or let sink down in your ears as Jesus said in Luke 9:44, will eventually come out your mouth.

Listen to yourself! Can you afford to have what you just said come to pass? If not, stop and correct it right then! Replace it with praise (Ephesians 5:4).

Here is something I believe will help you get all this together in your life. I have learned over the years to tie the confessing of the covenant promises of God to some natural

activity I'm already in the habit of doing. I tie it to something I do continually such as praying at meals, brushing
my teeth and getting in my car. I use those activities to trig-
ger confessions of faith, power and praise. This creates a
constant building of God's Word into my spirit.

It also creates a rejection when hell tries to set my tongue
on fire with something from death, sickness, disease and
disaster—things from which Jesus has redeemed us.

Take heed to what you hear. Use the supernatural power
of the Word of God to tame your tongue. Plant word-seeds of
faith day after day.

Open your mouth and start the process of your miracle
victory today!

Love,
Kenneth

April 1988

More About Taming Your Tongue

Dear Partner,

Gloria and I just arrived in Sydney, Australia, last night after a really good series of meetings in Auckland, New Zealand. My, how hungry the people here are for the Word. However, it's the same everywhere. People are crying out for reality and that reality is Jesus.

I want to thank you for praying for Gloria and me and the rest of our team as we travel. Your words of faith and power are far more important to what we do than any of us really know. As the Word says in Colossians 2:2, we are knitted together in spirit and in love. And at times like this I can really tell it.

In my last letter to you, I talked about words and the fact that words are the process starters of everything in our lives. The Lord has instructed me to use this letter to share some additional things with you in that same area.

It is of utmost importance that we, the Body of Christ, gain command of our tongues. Without our words of faith, not only are we weakened, but the rest of the world is in deep trouble. We *must* grow up and become stronger than ever in Jesus and in the strength of the Holy Ghost! Our voice is God's voice in the earth.

In order to be His voice in the world, we must set

ourselves to tame our tongues. That taming must first start at home in our personal lives. Once our words are under control there, our voice of faith to others will be strong.

What does it mean to "tame" our tongue?

In James 3:2, the Word says, *"If any man offend not in word, the same is a perfect [mature] man, and able also to bridle [or to take charge of] the whole body."* Taming the tongue means to speak at all times without offense to the Word. Most folks are in the habit of saying whatever crosses their minds until trouble comes. Then they rush to God and pray a few words and confess a few scriptures, hoping to get a miracle to change things.

We must learn, however, that God is telling us to bridle, or take complete charge, of the overall direction of our lives, by taking charge over every word we speak.

In James 3:13-14, the Word says that someone with wisdom will keep his mouth shut if he has bitterness or strife in his heart. "He glories not," or in other words, he doesn't allow pride to take over his tongue and say things that are crosswise to the truth (the Word). He refuses to hook his tongue to anything from the natural, devilish world.

Verse 17 tells what a wise man does instead. He hooks his tongue to the Word, which is "wisdom from above."

* **The Word is pure. It flushes out the bitter, or salt water, mentioned in verse 11.**

* **The Word will get rid of the bitterness and strife as it is spoken to God in prayer and to our own ears in praise and worship.**

* The Word will then bring peace to a heart that was troubled with bitterness and strife.

* The Word's gentleness calms and settles and casts out stress and anxieties.

* The Word is easy to be entreated. It has been given to us to be used.

* The Word is honored by the Holy Spirit to be for us and not against us.

* The Word is full of mercy from God.

* The Word is our Covenant with Him.

As we speak the tender mercies of the Word over a problem, our faith begins to rise up within us. We then release words of faith and plant seeds of power.

Those seeds then begin to grow up and become greater than the problems. They begin to bear fruit—fruit of deliverance, healing, miracles, love, joy and peace. Souls are drawn into the kingdom as Jesus is lifted up by the words of our mouth.

James 3:17 says that the Word is without hypocrisy. That means when we call things that be not as though they were, we're not lying or being hypocrites. We are not speaking lies or deceptions. We are speaking seeds of faith. The seeds that start the processes of God's operations in our lives will change our entire surroundings.

To tame the tongue, then, is to act on Colossians 3:17 that says, *"Whatsoever ye do in word or deed, do all in the name of the Lord Jesus, giving thanks to God and the Father by him."*

Get your Bible right now and look up these scriptures that tell the effect our words have on our lives: Psalms 103:5, 141:3; Proverbs 4:24, 12:18, 13:2-3, 15:4; Malachi 3:13; Matthew 12:36; Luke 6:45.

Now look at Psalm 39:1: *"I said, I will take heed to my ways, that I sin not with my tongue: I will keep my mouth with a bridle, while the wicked is before me."*

This is a prayer that I have prayed for myself and I urge you to include it in your prayers too. Let's pray it for ourselves and each other! Let's change the courses of our lives—spirit, soul and body—not for just one month or a few days, but for the rest of our lives. Regardless of what happens around us, let's speak in line with love and faith.

I hope this letter helps to open your thinking and answer some questions about words and the role that they play in our lives.

Read aloud the scriptures I listed. Get in the Word. Stay there. *"Draw nigh to God, and he will draw nigh to you"* (James 4:8).

Thanks again for your prayers and support. Gloria and I love you and pray for you every day—wherever we are.

Jesus Is Lord,
Ken

May 1988

Give the Devil a Scare

Dear Partner,

I want to share something with you in this letter that the Lord has shown me in just the last few days. It will thrill you and arm you with such spiritual strength, that persecution will never be able to hurt you again.

You're going to love this—so read it very carefully.

In recent times, the Body of Christ in the United States has proven to be soft in the area of persecution—especially where the tongues of men are concerned. Ministers have displayed their hurts and have cried before all the world about what the media, the devil and everybody else has said about them. Church members and ministry supporters have cried and carried on and, in far too many cases, have backed off from their commitments and involvements.

Many are ashamed to be numbered among those who are visible in God's works.

Jesus said, "You are blessed *when men revile you, and perse-cute you...and say all manner of evil against you falsely for my sake*" (Matthew 5:11). To tell you the truth, most of us don't really believe it when Jesus tells us we're blessed when we are persecuted. But if Jesus says we are blessed—then we are!

Why would persecution be a blessing?

To answer that we must first realize that men are not the

root of the problem. They are only the messengers. Evil comes from the evil one—Satan. He is the enemy (Ephesians 6:12).

Satan is the one behind *all* persecution. But why? Why does he persecute us?

The Word says that devils believe and *tremble* (James 2:19). And as Jesus ministered, devils said to him, "Have you come to *torment* us?" First John 4:18 says that *fear has torment.*

Persecution is an expression of Satan's terrible fear of us! Satan is filled with fear.

He flees when he is resisted by a believer in Jesus' Name. He is totally afraid of God, totally afraid of Jesus, and completely afraid of anyone who belongs to Jesus because *"greater is He that is within us than he that is in the world"* (1 John 4:4). He believes in and trembles at the righteousness of God, the power of the Word, and the authority in the Name of Jesus.

Mark 4:17 says persecution arises for the Word's sake. Satan knows that the believer has the same right to the powerful Word of God that Jesus has. He knows that once a person finds out who he is in Christ Jesus, and what all is available to him through the Word, that person of faith will begin to govern hell's affairs on this Earth the same way Jesus did in His earthly ministry.

No wonder Satan is so afraid of us! He has absolutely no defense. The only thing he can do is try, through persecution and affliction, to distract your mind from him as being the source of all your trouble.

We are the righteousness of God in Christ Jesus. We have every right before God that Jesus has. But Satan is working frantically to blind us to that truth. He is doing all he can to keep us preoccupied with what those who are unlearned and unskillful in the Word of righteousness are saying about us and doing to us. That way, we will not pay any attention to him and he'll be free to continue sowing sin and discord in the Body of Christ.

Don't let him succeed. Instead, do what Jesus said and *rejoice when men persecute you.* Rejoice! Why? Because our enemy is defeated! He knows it and he's terrified!

Turn the tables on Satan! Give him something to fear! Go to the Word of God, get the scriptures that cover your situation, then let him have it with both barrels! Don't let up! Pour it on! Stay with it day after day!

Satan has no defense against the Word.

Rejoice—and then hit him again!

Every time someone says something ugly, laugh out loud and rejoice again—again and again and again. Rejoice until you are so thrilled to belong to Jesus that no sickness, disease, lack or any such thing can stay nigh your dwelling.

You are righteous (2 Corinthians 5:17-21)!

You have the right to win with the Word, the Name of Jesus and the power of heaven!

Get with it and let the Word fight the fight! That's what the devil is so afraid you're going to do.

In closing this letter, I want to thank you so much for the way you pray and support this ministry. This whole work belongs to Jesus. You and I are Partners together with Him.

Gloria and I love you and pray for you daily.

In Jesus' Love,
Kenneth

June 1988

Don't Be So Problem-Minded That You Can't See the Victory!

Dear Partner,

God is moving! There are miracles at hand! Jesus is Lord and always will be!

I'm telling you, there is something stirring way down deep in my spirit. There's about to be a breakthrough in the Body of Christ in the power of the Holy Ghost.

Don't miss it by being problem-centered instead of being Jesus, victory, faith and Word of God-centered. Fill your eyes with Jesus once again by going back to the Word of His faith.

We are so surrounded with the loud voice of the world, that the vision of our victory in Jesus can be pushed out of the center of our thinking until the cares of this world begin to choke the Word, and it becomes unfruitful. When that happens, faith and power begin to subside and life begins to cave in on us from every side. Just crying about it and continuing to look at the woe that's set before us by Satan won't ever change that defeat. Feeling sorry for ourselves won't change it.

It's the Word in our lives that Satan is after. The Word is the only thing that will change our lives. We are Word people. We are born of the Word. We are fed by the Word. The Word is our Sword and it's our Life.

Twenty-four hours from now the circumstances in our lives could be totally changed. Remember in 2 Kings 7, when the land was filled with famine? God's Word came to Elisha and said 24 hours from now there will be plenty. How could that be? Everything looked so dark.

But God began to move. Things began to happen that no one expected. Men had no answers, but God had all the answers. He just made a few small changes—no big deal for Him—and the tables were turned.

I remember a message I heard Oral Roberts preach a few years ago from this same scripture. It is still alive in my spirit. He said, "Twenty-four hours from now you can be back on top."

Hallelujah! Jesus is our Victory! I don't care how bleak things may look.

The four lepers in 2 Kings 7 said, "Why sit we here till we die?" They were the key to God's plan for turning things around.

Follow their example. Don't just sit there. Rise up in faith. Stand on God's Word.

Get strong. Praise God out loud. Let the Word pour out of your mouth. Don't accept defeat. Fight for your life. Get mad at Satan. Cast him out. Get mad at that sickness. Get angry with poverty and start giving. Don't just sit there until you die.

If you think you're going to die anyway, go out with a blaze of glory. If I knew for certain I was going to die, I'd be giving God all the glory. I'd leave this world shouting praises to God and casting out the devil.

Before I close, I want to shout praise to God for all He's doing at KCM. Last night I couldn't go to sleep for thinking about all the things God has laid before us. Friend, Jesus is coming! We've got a job to do, and it's glorious!

Gloria and I need your prayers and support more than ever. Stay in there with us—*together* we can do all things through Jesus.

Well, I could go on and on because I love you all so much, but I must close. Rise up and be healed!

Love,
Kenneth

August 1988

Impossible Things
Are Possible With God

Dear Partner,

Have you ever looked around at the challenges in your life and been tempted to throw up your hands and quit? Have you ever wanted to say, "God, this situation is impossible!"

I have! I remember one time in particular. A number of years ago we had just held a fine, Holy Spirit-anointed series of meetings in Seattle, Washington. As usual, I had preached until I was almost physically exhausted.

Then I did something I know full well not to do. On the way home, I began to allow myself to think about how impossible it was for Gloria and me to do all that God had laid out before us. At first I resisted the thoughts, but they kept creeping back across my mind. I was tired and didn't bother to get my Bible and put a stop to them.

The more I entertained those thoughts, the more impossible everything seemed to be. By the time we got home, I was faithless, weak and so tired I was almost sick. I was so beaten down I could hardly pray. I became defensive toward everyone around me.

Even when I tried to stop this horrible situation, it seemed as though I was powerless.

The next day I listened to a tape by John Osteen. His

scripture text was Luke 18:27: *"The things which are impossible with men are possible with God."* I listened to the whole tape and still felt like I was in a pit.

All that day and even the next day, the same terrible scenes of defeat kept playing on the screen of my mind. Impossible! Impossible!

Then late in the afternoon, that scripture I had heard from Brother Osteen began to take root. It began to rise up on the inside. Deep down in my spirit, faith began to come forth.

I still felt really bad—not as bad as before, but bad enough. When I awoke the next morning, however, it was a different story!

The Word-seed of victory had worked all night. Faith was strong.

I then realized what had happened to Peter when he walked on the water in Matthew 14. He began to think about the fact that walking on water is impossible. That scared him so much that he lost sight of the fact that he was *already doing it!*

What was impossible with man was possible with God!

Just after I got out of bed the Lord spoke to me and told me to write what had happened in a letter to you. He directed me to write and let you know that Gloria and I aren't exempt from the pressures of life. We face them just like everyone else does. So when we say the Word works, we know what we're talking about. When we say there is victory in Jesus, it's because we have proven it out in our own lives. We've seen God do the impossible again and again.

My message to you today is this: *Stay with the Word. It will stay with you.*

Stay in faith! Put those thoughts of impossibility out now! Don't let them get started. Act out Proverbs 4:20-23:

"My son, attend to my words; incline thine ear unto my sayings. Let them not depart from thine eyes; keep them in the midst of thine heart. For they are life unto those that find them, and health to all their flesh. Keep thy heart with all diligence; for out of it are the issues of life."

1. **Attend to God's Word—put it first whether you like it or not.**

2. **Find your promise and force your mind to focus on it—not on the impossibility.**

3. **Believe the Word is life and health.**

4. **Protect yourself from doubt and unbelief.**

Whatever you have to do to shut off the voice of doom around you, *shut it off!*

Fill your ears with tapes. Fill your eyes with promise. Fill your mouth with praise. Do it now!

Let's join our faith together. We'll believe with you for your miracle victory, and you believe with us for ours. I really mean this. Let's go for it! Let's go after God's best and receive it!

Love,
Kenneth

October 1988

Sorrow Not!

Dear Partner,

Isaiah 51:11 says that sorrow shall flee away from the redeemed of the Lord.

In the past few years, Gloria and I have had two powerful opportunities to believe God's Word and stand against the spiritual force of sorrow. Once when Gloria's youngest brother went home to heaven very suddenly and again, when my mother went to be with the Lord.

We are here to report loud and clear that sorrow and grief do not stand a chance against the joy of the Lord. However, like everything in Jesus, a stand must be taken. Nothing is just automatic.

Why should we stand against grief and sorrow? Isn't feeling sad just the natural thing to do in certain situations? The very fact that it is the *natural* thing to do gives us our first clue to the importance of *not* allowing it into our lives.

However, there's much more to it than that. God's Word is very specific about it. First Thessalonians 4:13 just bluntly says, *"Sorrow not!"*

Isaiah 53 says Jesus bore our griefs and carried our sorrows. If Jesus was required to bear sorrow and defeat it on the cross, then it must be satanic. It must be designed to steal, kill and destroy. If you'll look up the Hebrew words translated *griefs and sorrows*, you'll find those same words can be translated sickness and weakness and pain. Grief and sorrow come from the same source as sickness, weakness and pain—*death!*

Grief and sorrow are death's ever-present, shadowing companions. That in itself lets us know they are not to be tolerated at any time.

One of the most dangerous aspects of grief and sorrow is their ability to choke the Word and cause it to become unfruitful in our lives. Without the Word alive in our hearts, we are helpless against the forces of darkness. Not only is the Word our sword, according to Ephesians 6:14-17, it serves as two other major pieces of our spiritual armor as well. We cannot do without it.

I didn't really realize how sorrow could steal the Word until I began to stand against it in faith. Then the Holy Ghost made it very plain to me that it fell under the category of *"the lusts of other things entering in"* in Mark 4:19. When we face painful situations, it's easy to begin to lust after that gush and rush of sorrowful emotion, to let it flood our soul taking over our will and mind. In a way, we actually enjoy all the attention, sympathy and such that goes along with it.

However, it's when all the "mourners" and "back patters" have gone home that grief and sorrow begin to do their real work. It's then that the awful pain and inward mental pressure comes. It's then that the overwhelming and seemingly unbearable loneliness and sadness crush in upon us. The misery of it goes on and on—to no good end.

The worst thing about all this is that the Church of Jesus Christ has the power and authority over sorrow. But instead of using that authority, we've yielded to sorrow's cold clammy arms of defeat. Well, no more!

What is sorrow? The dictionary defines it as "a heavy weight that comes from loss." Someone said to me, "I'm sorry to hear you lost your mother." I didn't lose her. I know where she is and she knows where I am. We're not lost.

Notice also it is a weight. Hebrews 12:1 tells us to lay aside *every* weight. "But Brother Copeland, I can't just lay aside this sorrow." Yes you can. Here's how:

1. **Remember that Jesus defeated sorrow and bore it for you.** It no longer has any real power over you, so all of its strength is coming from what you give it.

2. **Use the power of the Word.** The Word says don't sorrow! Whenever the Word tells you not to do something, it also provides you the power you need to obey it.

3. **Don't be fooled by your flesh.** Take a stand. At the first sign of depression, loneliness, tears or self-pity, stand up with the Word and fight back. Quote the Word aloud. "I sorrow not. I'm not a person without hope. I belong to Jesus and He has defeated grief and sorrow for me."

4. **Always see grief and sorrow as spirit beings— not just emotions.** They are personalities that want to take over your emotions and then take over your life. Stand up and fight them. You belong to Jesus, not to those two thieves!

5. **Begin to minister joy to others.** First Thessalonians
4:13-18 says, *"Comfort one another with these words."*
As you reach out to others, don't reach out in sympathy.
Reach out in the power of the Holy Spirit, our
Comforter. Break the power of those two devils, grief
and sorrow, with the Word and the Name of Jesus.
Don't let go.

Keep speaking the Word in love until those who are in
sorrow begin to take hold of it. Then they will begin to
stand with you. That's when the powerful force of joy, our
strength, begins to come like a flood. It takes over. Our emotions begin to get in line with the real thing. No more pain.
No more loneliness. We have Jesus! We have one another!
We have life! Let's shout!

I urge you to search your heart right now and see if you've
allowed sorrow to dwell there. What you find may surprise
you. You may discover, for instance, that you're still grieving
over things that happened years ago. Or you may find that
sorrow has gotten hold of you, not through major events,
but through seemingly small disappointments. You may
even be worrying and grieving over something that hasn't
even happened yet.

No matter what the source is, however, remember that
sorrow will drain you of life and strength every day.

So take a stand against it today. Make a commitment to
drive grief and sorrow away again and again with the Word
of God until they don't even try to come back anymore.

Don't put it off. Do it now!

You are so important to Gloria and me and all the rest of

us here at KCM. Your prayers are vitally important to all the other Partners. What's most important, though, is you are so important to Jesus and what He has set out to get done through this ministry. We love you so much.

I pray for you every day.

Your Brother in Christ Jesus,
Kenneth

November 1988

Start Releasing the Love

Dear Partner,

Things are really happening here at KCM!

Everyone has been caught up in a spirit of prayer and revival. *Everybody* is praying about *everything.* Even the very smallest of things—things that in the past would have gone unnoticed, are being prayed over with earnest expectation. All of us have decided that we want God's plan and purpose in every situation—large or small.

In all my years of ministry, I've never seen anything quite like it. Faith is flowing like a river along with a fresh, new atmosphere of God's love and power.

The reason I'm telling you all this is because you're very much a part of it. For if it hasn't already, this fresh, new wave of the Spirit is going to invade your life just like it has ours.

As Colossians 2:2 says, our hearts are knit together in love. The word translated love there is *agape.* That's the unconditional love of God that is brought to life when a blood covenant relationship has been established. We are covenanted together by the blood of Jesus. We are in Him and He is in us.

As Partners together in this ministry, you are partakers of my grace. The grace, power and blessing that God has given Gloria and me to carry out this assignment is available to you.

I know you are praying for me, and I earnestly expect our every need to be met through the Holy Ghost. At the same time, I'm praying for you every day in strength and power. I plead the blood of Jesus over you and declare you free every day of the world.

So stir up your expectancy. Take hold of the hope and faith that all of us here at KCM are releasing for you. Start looking for something fresh and exciting to happen every moment of every day. To me, there's a blessing just around the corner. That's the way I want it to be in your life also.

Throw fear out. Throw worry out. Bring in the joy. Start releasing the love *(agape)* that's been shed abroad in your heart by the Holy Spirit.

Love, love, love! My good friend Johnny Johnson says love is beyond defeat. The Bible says love *never* fails.

When you release love into a situation, you have released God. Think about that. When you release love into a situation, you have released God into that situation. Then Jesus becomes responsible for its success.

The Word of God is love.

The Name of Jesus is love.

The gifts of the Spirit are love.

The Blood of Jesus is love.

We are born of the Holy Spirit Who is love.

Heaven is love.

Love is heaven.

The person who refuses to love is missing out on the very best God has to offer.

Don't *you* miss out on any of it. Release love every

moment into every situation, every prayer and every thought until it totally consumes your life.

Go for it! It will strengthen you and cast out every fear that has robbed you of God's greater blessings. It will drive the devil out of your affairs and set you free from every torment of darkness.

Well, I could go on and on about this because this letter is being poured out of my spirit because of my love for you and Jesus. But I must close.

Love,
Kenneth

December 1988

Let's Have Christmas All Year

Dear Partner,

What a time of year Christmas is! It's the greatest time of all to win souls and put love into action.

During those few days every year people are tenderhearted. They're more open to giving and receiving than they are at any other time. That opens them up spiritually and puts them in a position to receive testimonies and ministry from you and me.

As you reach out to them in the days ahead, remember: Love and faith are the keys. When you're ministering the love of God with faith that the Word will not return void, you'll be irresistible to those with needs.

In light of that, I want to share something with you in this letter that will be a special blessing during the Christmas season—not only to you, but also to all the people around you as well. It will be a blessing to people you'll be sharing with who don't know Jesus as personally as you do.

You'll find it in Luke 2:13-14. There the Word of God says, *"And suddenly there was with the angel a multitude of the heavenly host praising God, and saying, Glory to God in the highest, and on earth peace, good will toward men."*

Notice these angels were praising God for a particular

reason. They were praising Him because peace was being declared between God and man, between heaven and Earth.

But wait a minute!

They were making the declaration at Bethlehem. Jesus was only a newborn baby at that time. How could peace be declared between God and man before Jesus had faced one test, before He had gone through even one temptation, before any battles for men had been fought, before one person was ever healed under His ministry? How could God send the angels to say such things when the battle for man's redemption was still 33 years away?

By faith, that's how!

As Romans 4:17 tells us, God calls things that be not as though they were. He had already set His faith on man's redemption. So, as far as He was concerned, it was done. He began treating men like they'd never sinned. He reached out to them in His great love. He totally offered Himself to man as though Jesus had already gone to the cross.

Because of God's faith and love, everything turned out perfectly. Jesus won every battle and took man away from Satan's authority and dominion.

Now, keeping all that in mind, I want you to think about something. If God acted as though the work of the cross had already been done before Jesus ever went to the cross, how do you think He is acting now?

He is acting as though we were already in Glory. He is saying that we've been raised up together and made to sit together in heavenly places in Christ Jesus. As far as our heavenly Father is concerned, you and I are already there!

So we need to start living that way! Where our needs are

concerned and where our relationship with God is concerned, we need to start living as though we're already seated with our Lord in Glory.

Let's begin to look at one another in Christ Jesus and treat one another like we were already in heaven. If we will, heaven will come down among us! After all, we all look a whole lot better in Jesus than any other way.

This can be the greatest Christmas any of us have ever had if we'll really get into making it great for someone else instead of just hanging around waiting for everyone to do something great for us. After all, it's Jesus' birth we're celebrating and not our own. So get that celebration off to a powerful start.

First, read the Christmas story in the Word again very carefully. Let it come alive and be real in your heart, and not just a fable.

Second, make giving your priority. Give, give, give. And don't just give things that can be bought! Give joy and peace and love. If things have gone wrong between you and someone else, take this opportunity to make them right.

Finally, take on the spirit of joy! The Word says joy to the world. Take on that joyous spirit. Spread it around everywhere you go. As you do these things, you'll begin to realize that your needs are being met even though that's not your primary goal. That's when it will dawn on you that this is not just a Christmas attitude, it's Jesus' attitude. It's an attitude you and I can have 12 months out of the year!

Isn't that great? Let's just stop right now and shout a praise to God for giving us Jesus!

Before I close, I want to tell you how grateful I am to you and to all of our Partners everywhere for being so faithful to pray and support Gloria and me with such power.

Gloria and I love you and pray for you every day.

Your Partner in Christ,
Kenneth

February 1989

Receive God's Blessings!

Dear Partner,

I want to share some prayer tips with you that I know will help you, especially in your praying for other people.

One of the most difficult areas of prayer comes when you want to pray for someone, but you don't know just what to pray except, *"God bless so-and-so."* Actually, that prayer means very little.

Ephesians 1:3 tells us that the Father has *already* released every blessing to us in heavenly places in Christ Jesus. So, a better way to pray would be, *"Father, have them receive all the blessings You have provided for them."*

You see, the problem is not getting God to bless people. He has already done His part. The problem is in their receiving what He has already provided.

You can see what I mean if you'll think about what happened when you were saved. God didn't have to do something at that time to "save" you. He did the "saving" 2,000 years ago. You just had to *receive* Jesus as Savior.

Well, the same thing is true with all the other benefits Jesus bought and paid for with His life's blood at Calvary!

But many of the people you're praying for don't know that they have already been blessed. They don't know what those blessings are or how to receive them. So praying for them is like praying for someone to receive what has been left to them in a will, and they don't even know it has been left to them.

They *are* blessed and they don't know it!

The answer to this dilemma is laid out for us in Ephesians 1, in the prayer that the Holy Spirit directed the Apostle Paul to pray for the people in the church there. As I pointed out, he told them in verse 3 that they were blessed already with all spiritual blessings in heavenly places. Then in verses 16-23, he told them how he prayed for them.

You can pray for yourself and others the same prayer Paul prayed. It is a Holy Ghost inspired prayer, therefore it is extremely effective. I pray it for my Partners all the time. Here it is:

Father, I pray for _____ right now; that You, the Father of Glory may give unto _____ the spirit of wisdom and revelation in the knowledge of Christ Jesus: That the eyes of _____'s understanding be enlightened, that _____ may understand what is the Hope of His calling, and what the riches of the glory of His inheritance is in the saints, and what is the exceeding greatness of His power toward _____ who believes according to the working of His mighty power, which He wrought in Christ, when He raised Him from the dead, and set Him at His own right hand in the heavenly places, far above every name that's named, not only in this world, but in the world to come: And has put all things under Jesus' and _____'s feet, and gave Jesus to be the head over all things to the Church, which is His body, the fullness of Him that filleth all in all.

those pressures were doing to me, than about the Scripture promises I was standing on.

I saw something, then, from what Jesus said in Matthew 6:24-25:

"No man can serve two masters: for either he will hate the one, and love the other; or else he will hold to the one, and despise the other. Ye cannot serve God and mammon. Therefore I say unto you, Take no thought for your life, what ye shall eat, or what ye shall drink; nor yet for your body, what ye shall put on. Is not the life more than meat, and the body more than raiment?"

Notice that immediately after Jesus said, *"No man can serve two masters,"* He said, *"Take no thought."* He was saying that we serve our thoughts!

Isaiah 55 tells us to forsake our thoughts and by the Word take God's thoughts. Second Corinthians 10:5 says to cast out thoughts that challenge the Word and bring into captivity every thought to the obedience of Christ. In other words, make your thoughts obey the Word.

My deliverance came when I realized that circumstances don't have to change before you can change your thoughts. In fact, the circumstances may not ever change until your thoughts are switched from wrong to right thinking.

I realize that's not easy to do, especially in the midst of heavy darkness and trial. (If it was easy, everybody would be doing it.) So, here are some things that will help you bring your thoughts into captivity.

1. **Realize that even if it seems impossible, God would not tell you to do something that you cannot do.**

2. **You don't have to do it alone.** You have the Word (God's thoughts). You have the Holy Spirit to strengthen you. You have the mind of Christ.

3. **Change what you're saying.** Speak the Word continually, even if you don't feel like it and even if it seems like you just can't believe it at the moment. Remember, faith comes by hearing and hearing by the Word of God.

4. **Don't stay on the defensive. Get on the offensive!** Attack the spirit that's trying to control your thoughts. Speak to it. Shout as loud as you can. You don't have to shout for the devil to hear you, but you may have to shout for *you* to hear you.

5. **Stay with it.** Stay right on top of your thoughts. Don't let your mind get away with a thing. Don't start thinking about other natural things just to "get your mind off your situation." That may help for a few minutes, but it's false help. Remember, the weapons of our warfare are not carnal but powerful through God for the pulling down of strongholds. That's what you're dealing with—a stronghold. Pull it down!

6. **Get around other people who are full of faith.** Get into a meeting where the Word is being preached—or call together faith friends and have a home meeting. Don't rehearse the problem over and over. That just reinforces the stronghold. Let the other people do the talking. Make yourself listen, even if it makes you angry at first. Join in with faith and resist darkness.

7. Praise God! Do whatever it takes to make yourself praise.

Look at Psalm 9:1-3. *"I will praise thee, O Lord, with my
whole heart; I will show forth all thy marvellous works. I
will be glad and rejoice in thee: I will sing praise to thy
name, O thou most High.* When mine enemies are turned
back, they shall fall and perish at thy presence."

That's why praising seems so hard to do at first. Satan knows
that if you do it, he'll have to turn back and fall at God's presence.

I remind you now of what the Apostle Paul said to the church
at Philippi in Philippians 4:9: *"Those things, which ye have
both learned, and received, and heard, and seen in me, do."*

These things won't do you any good if you won't do them! So
start right now. Yes! In Jesus' Name, *you* take over your thinking!

I want you to be free. But most importantly, Jesus wants
you to be free—and your freedom is bought and paid for in
His precious blood.

Gloria and I and our prayer staff pray for you every day.
You'll never be without prayer again.

We love you,
Ken

May 1989

I Believe I Receive!

Dear Partner,

I bring a report of victory on top of victory, faith on top of faith. All over the world people are coming alive to the Word of God!

You know, just about the time things look dark and you think nothing is happening, here comes Jesus with a whole new glory-filled move of the Holy Spirit. Miracles begin to flow again, people get born again, people receive their healings, and the ministry takes on a new energy of growth in all directions!

It's like a spiritual springtime when the trees take on new life after the winter and everything begins to bud and turn green. We've been through a hard winter spiritually, but thank God, a spiritual springtime is in the air.

Oh, how it pays to stay with the Word no matter how hard things get. It pays to stay in faith. After all, *"this is the victory that overcometh the world"* (1 John 5:4). I don't care how many tough circumstances the world brings against you, they're not tough enough to overcome faith in Jesus and His Word.

In this letter, I want to share a faith key with you that will help you unlock the treasure house of God's blessings and bring into physical manifestation the answer to your needs. It's found in Mark 11:24:

"Therefore I say unto you, What things soever ye desire, when ye pray, believe that ye receive *them, and ye shall have them."*

Notice Jesus' words, "Believe you receive." Those are key words.

Now look at what Jesus said to Jairus when someone told him his daughter was dead. Jesus said, *"Be not afraid, only believe"* (Mark 5:36).

Everyone knows there is power in believing, but how do you do it? Actually, it's so simple it's amazing.

Believing is an action word. It's not some kind of mental state no one can figure out. The key to it is the words *"believe you receive."*

Now just before Jesus told us in Mark 11:24 to believe that we receive, He told us in verse 23 that we "shall have whatsoever we say." Put those two together and you'll see what a powerful thing it is when you actually *say* that key phrase, *"I believe I receive."* Something happens in your spirit when you say those words.

I don't understand how it happens, but it does. I don't understand how my digestive system knows what to do when I swallow something, but it does. All those glands, my stomach and so forth immediately go into action when I swallow a bite of food. I don't have to make it happen. I don't have to feel it happen. It just happens. That's the way the body is made.

In much the same way, when you feed on God's precious promises and "swallow" them into your spirit by saying, "I believe I receive," faith is released. You don't have to make it happen. You don't have to feel it happen. It just happens. The reborn spirit is made that way.

When you constantly say with your mouth, "I believe I receive my healing," or "I believe I receive my financial needs met," and then quote the scriptures that back those things, faith is released to bring power to bear in the areas of those needs.

I like something I heard Dr. Kenneth Hagin say some years ago, *"Keep the switch of faith turned on."*

This is one of the ways Gloria and I keep the switch of our faith turned on. We *constantly* say, "I believe I receive to the glory of God the Father." We say that when we read the Word. We say that key phrase all the time!

We especially say it in the face of darkness when it looks like we're not receiving. When everything looks the worst, we say it the loudest. *I believe I receive!*

I believe with all my heart this is one of the kingdom's most important keys. Use it! It works! God wants you well and prosperous and so do we.

We pray for you every day.

Love,
Kenneth

June 1989

We're Back!

Dear Partner,

A few days ago during a meeting I was attending, the Spirit of God spoke to me and said, "You're back now. Don't let the devil weaken you and push you around like that anymore." He was talking about the serious blow the Body of Christ let the devil deal the moving of the Spirit over the last few years.

We are back! We're moving again. I'm not just talking about Kenneth Copeland Ministries either. I'm talking about the whole Body of Christ.

Thank God, Jesus doesn't fail!

If every Christian on Earth failed, the gates of hell would still not prevail against the Church, because Jesus is Head of the Church, and hell would still have to deal with Him. Regardless of how bad things look, we're still more than conquerors through Him!

We're back, so let's do a better job of staying in faith. Let's stay with the Word and remain steady in love and in spiritual things by putting our spiritual lives first.

Galatians 5:16 says, *"Walk in the Spirit and ye shall not fulfill the lust [or pressure] of the flesh."* We walk in the Spirit by walking in faith. We walk in love and faith by walking in the Word, by acting and talking as if the promises of God are *already* true.

They *are* already true. They are settled in heaven forever. We don't have to see some kind of manifestation in order to believe what God has already said is true. It's true now! Every word!

When we act and talk as if every word is already done, changes begin to take place. Our lifestyles become lifestyles of faith and love. They also become lifestyles of results. It begins to be obvious to others that God is working in our lives.

Jesus said it like this, *"He that doeth truth cometh to the light, that his deeds may be made manifest, that they are wrought in God"* (John 3:21).

I don't care how bad things get or how dark it seems, darkness can never put out the light of God's Word. The key then is to stay alive to His Word and keep His Word alive in us. Keep His light in us bright by keeping it first in our lives regardless of what happens.

Even when people fail, it doesn't mean the Word failed. Even if churches fail, it doesn't mean the Word failed. On the contrary, it means someone failed the Word.

Even when someone fails the Word, it doesn't mean that person has to remain a failure. No! A thousand times, no! Just put that failure behind you and get back on the Word. Do it now!

God's mercies are new every morning. The Word is always right where you left it. Jesus is always there. Get back on the Rock of your salvation. It's still as solid as it ever was.

Hallelujah! The Body of Christ is back! We are ready now to witness greater acts and outpourings of the

Holy Spirit's power than ever before. It has already begun. Shout the victory!

We love you and pray for you every day.

Love,
Ken

July 1989

Stir Yourself Up!

Dear Partner,

A while back, Gloria and I were in a meeting at Brother Jerry Savelle's ministry. As he was preaching, the Lord opened my eyes to something that was keeping me from receiving from Him. I want to share it with you in this letter.

Some time before I had gone out there, I'd realized that I needed to be stirred up in my spirit—not only in my personal life, but also in my ministry to you and others. I just wasn't where I needed to be. I had become lazy about my faith and had let a don't-care attitude and lack of diligence begin to work its way into my life.

The Word says in 2 Peter 1:5-10, if this happens, you'll fall or stumble. With the added responsibility of our daily TV broadcasts and all the demands that have arisen from that, I knew something had to happen or I wasn't going to be able to carry out the assignment the Lord had given me to do. I began to pray, *"Lord, stir me up. Rise up inside me."*

Nothing happened.

If anything, I grew worse. Things became harder. I grew more and more tired physically. I could tell I was missing it somewhere. Somehow things just didn't click.

Then, that evening Brother Jerry began to preach about

the very situation I just described. He read 2 Timothy 1:6. *"Wherefore I put thee in remembrance that thou stir up the gift of God, which is in thee...."*

That verse hit me like a ton of bricks. *What's the matter with me?* I thought. *I knew that!*

I went over that scripture again in my mind. *"I remind you,* you *stir up the gift of God which is in thee."* The truth of it rang in my spiritual ears. *Stir yourself up! The Holy Spirit is already stirred up. Now stir yourself up to take hold of Him. You already know how. You do it by faith— not by feelings.*

I immediately said, "Thank you, Jesus. I stir myself up. I take hold in Jesus' Name. I receive strength in my inner man by the Spirit of God which is in me. I am *now* stirred up."

I walked out of that meeting saying to everyone, "I'm stirred up." I said it like I was stirred up. I acted stirred up. I said it to Gloria on the way home. I've been saying it ever since. Every time that laziness of spirit started coming on me, I said, "Oh no you don't. I'm stirred up. I'm strengthened by the Holy Spirit in my inner man! Thank God, the Word works! Faith works! I am stirred up!"

When I began praying about this letter, I got stirred up about your getting stirred up. Then the Lord instructed me to begin praying Ephesians 3:14-21 for you and all our other Partners:

¹⁴For this cause I bow my knees unto the Father of our Lord Jesus Christ,

¹⁵Of whom the whole family in heaven and earth is named,

¹⁶That he would grant you, according to the riches of his glory, to be strengthened with might by his Spirit in the inner man;

¹⁷That Christ may dwell in your hearts by faith; that ye, being rooted and grounded in love,

¹⁸May be able to comprehend with all saints what is the breadth, and length, and depth, and height;

¹⁹And to know the love of Christ, which passeth knowledge, that ye might be filled with all the fulness of God.

²⁰Now unto him that is able to do exceeding abundantly above all that we ask or think, according to the power that worketh in us,

²¹Unto him be glory in the church by Christ Jesus throughout all ages, world without end. Amen.

Take hold of that prayer for yourself. Take it by faith. Stir up the gift that is in you.

Eternal life is in you. Stir it up!

Faith is in you. Stir it up!

Love is in you. Stir it up!

Say this out loud, or even shout it out loud: *"I'm stirred up. And watch out, Mr. Devil, the faith bunch is on the move again."*

Praise God, a revival of His power is upon us and among us. It will flow according to the power that works within us!

We love you.

> Your Stirred Up Brother and Partner,
> Kenneth

P.S. We're already praying that prayer from Ephesians 3 for you and our other Partners every day. You add it to your prayers for us too. And remember, all you need is already in you now. Stir it up!

September 1989

Become Skillful in the Word of Righteousness

Dear Partner, Champion, Greatly Blessed of God, Joint Heir of Jesus,

I'm learning more every day of my life about what the Apostle Paul meant when he said, *"I thank my God upon every remembrance of you"* (Philippians 1:3). Lately it seems that I think about you all the time. Ministering to you and the rest of the Partners the Lord has given me has become foremost in my life and ministry.

Today, I want you to look with me at some verses in the book of Hebrews:

> 2:1 **Therefore we ought to give the more earnest heed to the things which we have heard, lest at any time we should let them slip.**
>
> 4:1 **Let us therefore fear, lest, a promise being left us of entering into his rest, any of you should seem to come short of it.**
>
> 4:2 **For unto us was the gospel preached, as well as unto them: but the word preached did not profit them, not being mixed with faith in them that heard it.**

[5:12]For when for the time ye ought to be teachers, ye have need that one teach you again
which be the first principles of the oracles of
God; and are become such as have need of
milk, and not of strong meat.

Notice, the people this scripture was written to had at
one time come to the place where they should have been
teachers. Then they slipped back until they needed baby
food again. It's easy to see what the problem was when you
read Hebrews 1-5. They let other things get in the way of
mixing faith with the Word. They let the promises slip, so
they slipped.

That's happened to a multitude of believers in the last
several years.

"Well, Brother Copeland," they've said, "We're tired of
that faith stuff." Or, "We just don't have time to spend that
much time in the Word," and so forth.

We all know where that leads:

Low Word Level=Low Faith Level=Slip

Then defeat comes in some area where there was once
victory in Christ Jesus.

Lately, the Lord has been dealing with me about the danger of slipping when everything is on the move again. Right
now God is moving everywhere! Lives are being changed.
Strongholds of darkness are being broken again. The
excitement is back in our church services and in our meetings, and multiplied thousands of people are coming
to Jesus.

When that happened in the 70s and early 80s, we all had the time of our lives. But then when it came time to grow and stand our ground, instead of locking into all we had learned and fighting the good fight of faith, too many of us slipped.

Why? Because we were riding the tide of blessing instead of digging deeper into what God had for us!

Well, we are rapidly coming to that glorious place again where the Word is so sweet we can't get enough of it, where the meeting tapes are greater than ever and where Christian fellowship is the greatest thing going. Let's don't just ride the tide of blessing.

Let's totally give ourselves to the One it is all about—Jesus, Head of the Church, our soon-coming King! Let's become mature believers like those mentioned in Hebrews 5:13-14—believers who can handle the meat of the Word.

"For every one that useth milk is unskillful in the word of righteousness: for he is a babe. But strong meat belongeth to them that are of full age, even those who by reason of use have their senses exercised to discern both good and evil."

Think about that! Think about becoming skillful in the Word of righteousness, learning how to live in our place of right-standing with the Almighty God, Possessor of heaven and Earth, growing up into Him in all things (Ephesians 4:15) and becoming full-grown, powerful, spiritual adults, not only with our own needs met, but also anointed to reach out and help meet the needs of others.

That's my greatest desire—to see all my Partners grow along with Gloria and me to greater and greater heights and abilities, to reach more and more broken souls with the fact that Jesus is alive and His Word works.

I urge you to read Hebrews 1-5 at least three times the next few days. Read it in the *New King James Version* and *The Amplified Bible* translations, as well as the *King James Version.*

Your faith will be "boiling over" and Satan and his bunch will be crying, "Oh no! Not again!" Then you'll let him have it with both barrels and rise up in great victory. Let's shout!

We're getting more victory reports of praise to Jesus for what He's doing in lives than ever in the history of this ministry. Many times more! To God and His Word go the glory.

This also means growth, growth, growth, in every area. But, praise God, faith works! Giving works! Our income has kept us up with the growth because of the prayers and the giving of Partners like you.

I'm believing for your blessing and income to increase too. We are in this together, and it's working!

Gloria and I and all of us here at KCM love you and pray for you every day.

Love,
Kenneth

December 1989

Obedience Is Greater Than Sacrifice

Dear Partner,

What a time we live in! Destruction and despair on one hand and revival and miracles on the other. Great pressure is being applied to the minds of men—pressure that is heavier and more oppressive than anyone alive on the Earth has ever seen before. It's driving people to do things they never dreamed they would ever do.

No one would ever drive their car over a cliff, passing sign after sign that said, *"Danger. Road Out. Stop!"*—unless they were not seeing the signs or were reading them wrong. That's what's happening today. People are not thinking straight. They're being blinded by depressed, fear-filled, pressure-affected minds.

But, praise God, born-again, Spirit-filled Christian people do not have to succumb to that darkness. We have the Word of faith!

Isaiah 54:13-17 says fear and oppression and terror will come, but not from the Redeemer. Fear and oppression have caused the destruction and the pressure we've been seeing around us. But, according to the Word, they're weapons against the redeemed that cannot prosper.

During times like these, it is ever so important for us to

spend time in prayer and in the Word so we can be led by the Master, Jesus, instead of being pushed around by the pressures of life. For instance, the great pressure of finances is on everyone everywhere in some form or another.

Financial pressure has gotten so great everywhere that governments don't know what to do. Businesses don't know what to do. Families don't know. Churches don't know. But Jesus does! Don't try to do anything without hearing from Him.

God has commissioned Jesus and anointed Him Lord over the time and the finances of the Body of Christ. However, instead of listening to Him, too many of God's people are being influenced by outside pressures—pressures that are stronger today than ever before.

*Pressure from traditions...*that causes us to just do what we've always done instead of following the leadership of the Holy Spirit. Traditions have made many believers content to just hand out a few tokens here and there that do little to nothing where the work of God and real needs are concerned.

*Pressure from the media...*that makes the lifestyle of giving look absurd—especially when that giving is to the Church or to the mission field or to ministries of any kind.

*Pressure from ministries...*that has misguided as much or maybe even more of God's goods than any of the other pressures. I know that this has harmed our work over the years more than any other one thing.

For example, as you know, our going on daily television greatly increased our operating budget. Now, we didn't go on more television to increase our assets or our income. We didn't do it to raise money. We went on TV to take God's Word to His people.

We stayed before God for several years until we were absolutely sure it was God's will to start the daily broadcast. Then as we stepped out and began to expand, of course, our expenses began to increase. However, so did our income. Then after a few months, our income leveled off—but the expenses kept rising.

We began to fall behind until we had to stop expanding, long before we finished what Jesus, Head of the Church, wanted us to do at that point!

Traditionally, this would have been the time to go into appeals on television and letters and really put the pressure on people, but we are not allowed to do that. Nowhere in the Word of God does it tell any ministry of any kind to put pressure on people.

We went before the Master and stayed there until we found out where we had missed His directions, and then we changed some things. We had some changing to do in our own house as a ministry and in our own lives personally. After doing all that, we were still $3 million short.

So we stayed before the Lord until we found out why.

Mostly it was because so many people are not worshiping God and not taking time to listen to Jesus' directions in their giving and receiving.

Since Gloria and I didn't get on television and talk about our needs all the time, then when God sent His angels and

His Spirit to speak to those people about what to do, they reasoned away the prompting of the Spirit by saying, "Kenneth doesn't need this. He never talks about money, so he must have all he can use. I've heard they give away millions of dollars, so they must have plenty. I'll give this over here or over there because they need it so badly."

Now please don't misunderstand me. I'm not saying this to criticize or to take away from other ministries. God forbid! I'm simply saying that too many people have not been doing what it takes to find out from the Master what He wants done. That's a large part of the reason ministries are behind so much of the time.

If everyone would listen to Jesus and do what He says, then all of us would have more than enough to do whatever He says to do. Our giving would be blessed instead of cursed. The works of God would go forth and the power of darkness would be broken over not only the Body of Christ, but also over the world as the Word goes forth in power.

God's Word is the most important thing in this earth. It is the answer to all the darkness, all the pressure, all the drugs and all the heartache we see around us. Jesus—the Word—cannot fail to overcome all the death and destruction that's going forth in this earth at Satan's hands. Why?

Get this now. Jesus is God's most perfect and precious seed.

Think about the importance of seeds for a minute. In Mark 4:30-32, when Jesus wanted to compare the kingdom of God to something, He compared it to a seed. Since everything comes from the kingdom of God, there is nothing that exists that didn't come from a seed. You were born from a seed. Then you were born again from the seed of God's Word. Your food and everything else comes from a seed.

Jesus Himself was "The Seed" planted by God. God sowed Him in sacrifice. He came forth and is still growing up into many brethren. The kingdom—or seed—cannot be stopped. It will grow up and become greater.

That's the reason Satan and the forces of darkness want to drain you until you can't plant your seed in His Name.

I understand the dollar-by-dollar draining and heaviness of the flesh and mind that you, and most everyone else, are going through. Payments for this, payments for that try to drain the very life and faith out of your heart. We've been there!

What's the answer to a situation like that? Plant more seed! And as you do it, worship and praise God with all your heart. (See Philippians 4:16-19.)

Your money—or goods—is the husk of the seed. Your words of faith, worship and love are the life in the seed. Regardless of what happens to the husk—or money—the life of the seed is spiritual and it is forever. It will grow until it breaks the powers of darkness and lack.

There *is* pressure and darkness all around us these days. And we've all allowed it to affect us to some degree. But we have taken steps of faith and power and we will overcome the effects of it in this ministry—and, praise God, you can do the same thing in your own life!

In Jesus' Name, I take authority over any darkness that has attacked you and your household in any way. I stand in faith with you believing that no weapon formed against you will prosper.

Please join Gloria and me and all of us at KCM in standing against the spirit of lack. Pray with us! Stand with us. Jesus can't fail, so we won't fail. We're staying close to Him. As you stand with us, we're standing with you.

Together—you, us and Jesus. What a team!

We love you and pray for you every day. Victory is ours.

Ken

January 1990

Rejoice! Jesus Is Coming!

Dear Partner,

Rejoice. And again I say rejoice.

Do it! Right now! I don't care what circumstances look like. I don't care if your insides are so tight you feel as if your jaw would break if you smiled. Open your mouth and rejoice.

Jesus is coming! Not only that, He's here now in the mighty person and presence of the Holy Spirit. So rejoice. Jesus sent Him to *you*. All He is, He is for *you*. All He has is *yours*. This is good news, so shout about it!

I have something I can hardly wait to share with you. We're all so excited about it, we can hardly stand it.

On Sunday morning, June 4, 1989, here at Eagle Mountain Church, just as we began to finish our worship and praise, the spirit of prophecy came on me and said some things to our congregation. They were exciting and thrilling, but they seemed like they were almost out of reach—*until six months later!* Read the prophecy and you'll see what I mean:

There is coming for you a great outpouring of the supernatural. Not just to bless the Church, but to cause a great awakening throughout the earth and in all lands, in all tongues, and all peoples in order to gather the precious fruit of the earth. For the time is at hand for all things written to be fulfilled.

The time is come and now is, saith the Lord, for great, great, great manifestations. Far beyond anything that has happened in the past. Not just beyond, but far beyond anything that has happened before.

Now this is what the Lord is saying, so hearken and heed to it. Listen. For a mighty wave of the supernatural is coming and soon to burst on the scene. Soon to crash like a mighty tidal wave and burst on the scene. Not just here and there and a little here and a little over there, but as a mighty wave splashes and covers entire continents.

And the power of God will rise up in places where people didn't even know that there was a God. But it will be there. There will be things that will fall before the pressure of it. People will shake their heads and say, "I never would have believed that could happen."

There are going to be political walls and political fences that crumble right before men's eyes. Mighty, mighty strongholds of political power and political strength in different political systems all over the world will suddenly change hands, crumble and fall, and men will say, "I never would have thought that would happen, but I'm seeing it. I'm looking at it."

THE BERLIN WALL WILL COME DOWN. IT'S A SIGN.

The Berlin Wall will come down. There will be other walls that will come down. There will be some walls that will go up. Many changes are going to take place. But those that are wise in their hearts and listen to the Spirit of God will be quick to say, "Oh, the Lord is at work in the land." And they will be quick to pray. And they will be quick to rise up as a witness in the streets, and they'll be quick to testify wherever they go, "The Lord is working! The Lord is working! He'll save you! He'll heal you! He'll deliver you! He'll bring you into the place that you ought to be."

Now, I'm not preparing you for a long time of comfort. I'm preparing you for a short time of supernatural outpouring. For the end is at hand. The end is at hand.

No, it's not an end for you, it's a beginning. The beginning of all you've longed for. The beginning of all that I've longed for, says the Spirit of Grace. The beginning, the starting, with the very first time in all things that My family will be in one place at one time with Me, all of us rejoicing and praising together.

So rejoice again, says the Lord. The time is at hand, and I'm more thrilled than you are about it. Hallelujah. Praise the Lord. And again, praise the Lord.

Remember now, this prophecy came forth back in June of 1989. It was totally wild and unreasonable then to even think about the Berlin Wall coming down. But six months later, it did!

Man, when God begins to move, it doesn't matter what men have built, He can change it in a day!

Do you recall when the man of God prophesied in 2 Kings 7:1, *"Tomorrow about this time shall a measure of fine flour be sold for a shekel [or just a few cents]"?* When that prophecy came forth, there was no flour available at any price. There was a famine so deep and hard in the land that people were becoming cannibals and eating their children.

It was a terrible situation, almost beyond men's minds to conceive. Right in the middle of all of that, the man of God said, "In 24 hours, things will be entirely different."

It sounded impossible, but it happened. It sounded just as impossible when the Lord said, "There are going to be political walls and fences that crumble right before men's eyes." It sounded impossible, but it has happened right before our eyes as we watched them crumble on television.

Think about your own impossible situation in the light of all this. It should encourage you like it has encouraged Gloria and me. If God can bring down the Berlin Wall and flatten communism overnight, then our little problems don't stand a chance in the face of such power and outpouring. He said in that prophetic word that the power of God will rise up and things will fall before the pressure of it. Then He said, "Be quick to say, 'The Lord is at work in the land. The Lord is working.'"

He will bring you into the place where you ought to be. Start saying that. Say it over and over every day, "The Lord is at work in my situation. He's bringing me into the place I ought to be. He's delivering me now."

This is not the time to sit on the sidelines and just try to get comfortable. It's time to commit all we have to Jesus and His Work. It's time to seek His face for His perfect will and then carry it out with all our might. It's time to plow our finances, talents, time, our all in all, into the preaching of the gospel to every creature.

Let's go forth with all our strength and with all of the force of faith within us with the message of God's faith and love in Jesus. Together, we can do all things through Christ (the Anointed One and His anointing) which strengthens us.

Gloria and I love you and pray for you every day. Jesus is Lord!

Love,
Kenneth

June 1990

Press On in Prayer

Dear Partner,

Are you where you want to be spiritually? If you are, have you determined your next goals?

This is certainly not the time to relax in your faith. Nor is it a time to get down on yourself if things haven't worked out like you wanted. The Apostle Paul said, "I forget those things that are past and press on."

Today I want you to take a look at the scriptures we here at KCM are praying for you. I also want to urge you to include these scriptures in your prayers for us. Many of our Partners already do and I know without a doubt that their prayers are having a powerful impact on us. This ministry is in the best condition spiritually and otherwise that it has ever been since the day of its beginning in 1967. I know that we would never have come this far without the prayers of our Partners—prayers based on Psalm 103, Ephesians 1:16-23, Ephesians 3:14-20 and Colossians 1:9-11.

Praise God, the Word works! So let's press forward and keep putting it to work in our prayers and in every area of our lives!

Let's begin by looking at Psalm 103:

[1]Bless the Lord, O my soul: and all that is within me, bless his holy name.

[2]Bless the Lord, O my soul, and forget not all his benefits:

[3]Who forgiveth all thine iniquities; who healeth all thy diseases;

[4]Who redeemeth thy life from destruction; who crowneth thee with lovingkindness and tender mercies;

[5]Who satisfieth thy mouth with good things; so that thy youth is renewed like the eagle's.

[6]The Lord executeth righteousness and judgment for all that are oppressed.

[7]He made known his ways unto Moses, his acts unto the children of Israel.

[8]The Lord is merciful and gracious, slow to anger, and plenteous in mercy.

You know, we can get so problem centered that we become part of our own problem. Don't let that happen. Speak to your soul, your mind, will and emotions. Tell yourself daily to recall *all* God's benefits. Forgiveness of sins, healing, protection, redemption, deliverance and restoration in every area of life—all these things belong to us in Jesus. Think about these benefits instead of the problems that surround you.

Then remember that I pray all these benefits for you *every day*. So does the KCM staff.

Now let's look at another scripture we pray for you, Ephesians 1:16-23:

[16][I] cease not to give thanks for you, making mention of you in my prayers,

[17]That the God of our Lord Jesus Christ, the Father of glory, may give unto you the spirit of wisdom and revelation in the knowledge of him:

[18]The eyes of your understanding being enlightened; that ye may know what is the hope of his calling, and what the riches of the glory of his inheritance in the saints,

[19]And what is the exceeding greatness of his power to us-ward who believe, according to the working of his mighty power,

[20]Which he wrought in Christ, when he raised him from the dead, and set him at his own right hand in the heavenly places,

[21]Far above all principality, and power, and might, and dominion, and every name that is named, not only in this world, but also in that which is to come:

[22]And hath put all things under his feet, and gave him to be the head over all things to the church,

[23]Which is the body, the fulness of him that filleth all in all.

Since the Apostle Paul said he prayed this for the church members at Ephesus, I pray it for you by putting "my

Partners" every place it says "you" in the prayer. Then I believe I receive each part of the prayer myself because I know many of my Partners are also praying it for me.

Next, let's read Ephesians 3:14-20. It falls right in behind 1:16-23 and brings the power of the Holy Spirit and all of His might, His ability, into our lives.

¹⁴For this cause I bow my knees unto the Father of our Lord Jesus Christ,

¹⁵Of whom the whole family in heaven and earth is named,

¹⁶That he would grant you, according to the riches of his glory, to be strengthened with might by his Spirit in the inner man;

¹⁷That Christ may dwell in your hearts by faith; that ye, being rooted and grounded in love,

¹⁸May be able to comprehend with all saints what is the breadth, and length, and depth, and height;

¹⁹And to know the love of Christ, which passeth knowledge, that ye might be filled with all the fulness of God.

²⁰Now unto him that is able to do exceeding abundantly above all that we ask or think *according to the power that worketh in us.*

Read that last sentence again. Man, that's shoutin' ground! All of that great ability is at work *inside us!* Hallelujah!

Now let's go to Colossians 1:9-11:

⁹For this cause we also, since the day we heard it, do not cease to pray for you, and to desire that ye might be filled with the knowledge of his will in all wisdom and spiritual understanding;

¹⁰That ye might walk worthy of the Lord unto all pleasing, being fruitful in every good work, and increasing in the knowledge of God;

¹¹Strengthened with all might, according to his glorious power, unto all patience and long-suffering with joyfulness.

This scripture makes it clear that God is planning on all of us bearing fruit and being successful in *every* good work. Not just barely getting by, but increasing in God's knowledge during these days when everything around us, from banks to churches, is folding up and failing because no one knows what to do.

But Jesus knows! And if He knows, we can find out and then give Him the glory for the success.

That's what we are praying for you, our Partners, every day. Not just when we think about it, but *every* day, 365 days a year. You *are* being prayed for.

Don't ever forget it. Stand on it in faith.

I am certainly standing on the prayers and faith of my Partners. I'm depending on them. Together, we can do anything God asks us to do.

We all love you more and more each day in Christ Jesus.

Love,
Kenneth

July 1990

Agree With Jesus

Dear Partner,

Jesus is Lord and great grace is upon us!

This ministry is really on the move. There are so many good reports and faith victories that there's not enough room in this letter to even start sharing them with you. One step at a time, one victory then another, steadily gaining speed and momentum, we've overcome and set aside the hardships that Satan has hurled at us.

The Word works! The Lord liveth and prayer changes things!

Speaking of prayer, I want us to take a close look at a very powerful prayer that Jesus prayed just before He went to the cross. Since He was not praying for Himself, but was praying for you and me, we should be very careful to agree with Him and receive from the Father what Jesus asked Him to give us. You'll find this prayer in John 17:1-26:

[1]These words spake Jesus, and lifted up his eyes to heaven, and said, Father, the hour is come; glorify thy Son, that thy Son also may glorify thee:

[2]As thou hast given him power over all flesh,

that he should give eternal life to as many as thou hast given him.

[3]And this is life eternal, that they might know thee the only true God, and Jesus Christ, whom thou hast sent.

[4]I have glorified thee on the earth: I have finished the work which thou gavest me to do.

[5]And now, O Father, glorify thou me with thine own self with the glory which I had with thee before the world was.

[6]I have manifested thy name unto the men which thou gavest me out of the world: thine they were, and thou gavest them me; and they have kept thy word.

[7]Now they have known that all things whatsoever thou hast given me are of thee.

[8]For I have given unto them the words which thou gavest me; and they have received them, and have known surely that I came out from thee, and they have believed that thou didst send me.

[9]I pray for them: I pray not for the world, but for them which thou hast given me; for they are thine.

[10]And all mine are thine, and thine are mine, and I am glorified in them.

[11]And now I am no more in the world, but these are in the world, and I come to thee. Holy Father, keep through thine own name those whom thou hast given me, that they may be one, as we are.

[12]While I was with them in the world, I kept them in thy name: those that thou gavest me I have kept, and none of them is lost, but the son of perdition; that the scripture might be fulfilled.

[13]And now come I to thee; and these things I speak in the world, that they might have my joy fulfilled in themselves.

[14]I have given them thy word, and the world hath hated them, because they are not of the world, even as I am not of the world.

[15]I pray not that thou shouldest take them out of the world, but that thou shouldest keep them from the evil.

[16]They are not of the world, even as I am not of the world.

[17]Sanctify them through thy truth: thy word is truth.

[18]As thou hast sent me into the world, even so have I also sent them into the world.

[19]And for their sakes I sanctify myself, that they also might be sanctified through the truth.

[20]Neither pray I for these alone, but for them also which shall believe on me through their word;

[21]That they all may be one; as thou, Father, art in me, and I in thee, that they also may be one in us: that the world may believe that thou hast sent me.

²²And the glory which thou gavest me I have given them; that they may be one, even as we are one:

²³I in them, and thou in me, that they may be made perfect in one; and that the world may know that thou hast sent me, and hast loved them, as thou hast loved me.

²⁴Father, I will that they also, whom thou hast given me, be with me where I am; that they may behold my glory, which thou hast given me: for thou lovedst me before the foundation of the world.

²⁵O righteous Father, the world hath not known thee: but I have known thee and these have known that thou hast sent me.

²⁶And I have declared unto them thy name, and will declare it: that the love wherewith thou hast loved me may be in them, and I in them.

Let's first notice verse 20 so that we are assured Jesus is praying for us today, and not just for those who were present with Him when He prayed this prayer: *"Neither pray I for these alone, but for them also which shall believe on me through their word."*

Every one of us was born again either directly or indirectly through the words of Jesus' disciples. So we are definitely included in this prayer. What's more, if you take the time to study out the things that I'm going to point out to you, you'll find that what we see in this prayer is also promised in other scriptures throughout the Bible.

As you look at these things Jesus prayed, pray along with Him and receive what He requested.

In verse 11, Jesus asked the Father to keep us in His Name while we are in the world. He asked that we be kept and protected from evil (verse 15). Then in verse 16 we get some insight into how this is to be done. It says we *are not of the world, even as I [Jesus] am not of the world.*"That means the world and its evil has no authority over us. We have authority over it in His Name. We are of His Name, not of this world.

Jesus brings the Word into the picture in verse 17: *"Sanctify them through thy truth: thy Word is truth."* The word sanctify simply means to separate. Thank God, His Word will separate us from sin, sickness, demons, fear, poverty and all that evil has to bring against us.

In verse 13, Jesus asked that His joy be fulfilled in us. This is the same joy spoken of in Hebrews 12:2 that was set before Him before the cross and was so powerful that the promise of it carried Him all the way through crucifixion, death, hell and then resurrection.

The joy of the Lord *is* our strength! It's the joy of having overcome death and having totally defeated Satan and hell! That is the joy He has now at the Father's right hand and it is ours. It is yours right now!

Let's go now to verse 24. There, Jesus asked the Father for us to be given joint status with Him in the Father's presence. We know by reading Ephesians 2:6 that this has been granted. It says we've been raised up with Him and made to sit with Him in heavenly places.

That's great, but it's not all Jesus prayed for us.

He also asked that we have a revelation of the glory the Father had given Him. The foundation of that glory was and is the great all-that-the-Father-has-and-is kind of love God has for Jesus. The love that was before the foundation of the world. Jesus asked that we be given insight into it.

Read Ephesians 1:17-19. (It's part of the prayer that we pray for our Partners daily.)

> [17]That the God of our Lord Jesus Christ, the Father of glory, may give unto you the spirit of wisdom and revelation in the knowledge of him:
> [18]The eyes of your understanding being enlightened; that ye may know what is the hope of his calling, and what the riches of the glory of his inheritance in the saints,
> [19]And what is the exceeding greatness of his power to us-ward who believe, according to the working of his mighty power.

Now reread verses 21-23 of Jesus' prayer.

> [21]That they all may be one; as thou, Father, art in me, and I in thee, that they also may be one in us: that the world may believe that thou hast sent me.
> [22]And the glory which thou gavest me I have given them; that they may be one, even as we are one:

^{23}I in them, and thou in me, that they may be
made perfect in one; and that the world may
know that thou hast sent me, and hast loved
them, as thou hast loved me.

When we agree with Jesus and begin to seek His revelation, then and only then will the unity Jesus prayed for
come to pass. Why? This oneness Jesus is referring to
comes from inside the spirit of believers. It can never come
by organizing and all the other things men try to do to get it
to come to pass. These things are not necessarily wrong and
in some cases they help, but there is yet to come a glorious
revelation of the awesome, all-encompassing love with
which God the Father loves Jesus. When that revelation
fills the hearts of the believers, we will at last see true unity
in the Body of Christ.

In verse 26, Jesus said He would not cease declaring His
Name to us, anointing members of His Body to keep teaching and preaching until we receive the glorious revelation
that the love wherewith God loves Jesus is now in us. He
not only loves us with that same love, but has shed it abroad
and deposited it in our hearts so we can use it to love
one another!

The very thought of that staggers the mind, doesn't it? No
wonder it has to come by revelation of the Holy Spirit!

It is God Himself! Bigger than all things! The God of
heaven and Earth, creator of life, giver of existence, is *love!*

Look at verse 21 and see what will happen when this
revelation finally explodes in the hearts of believers. It says

the world will then believe that Jesus was sent from God. Evangelism will be no problem. The gospel will be preached as a witness to all nations and then the end shall come.

I believe with all my heart this is about to happen. We all know that these are the last of the last days. I believe this revelation of God's glorious love is at hand.

What can we do to lay hold of this revelation for ourselves?

To start with, act on the first part of verse 21. Jesus has given us His glory, the Father's love. So receive it. Claim it. It's yours. You have a right to revelation and insight into it. Receive and claim that by laying hands on these verses and saying:

Thank You, Jesus, it's mine now. Father, in Jesus' Name, open the eyes of my understanding and flood my spirit with the revelation of Your glorious love. Then show me how to love with that love the same way You love Jesus and me.

Now begin to practice that love every day. Surround others with love thoughts. Pick out certain people to be targets of your love and faith.

You and all the other Partners are targets of Gloria's and my love, love thoughts and prayers of faith.

We love you and pray for you every day.

Love,
Kenneth

August 1990

Be a Doer of the Word

Dear Partner,

To God be the glory! This ministry is completely debt free. We give great thanks and joy-filled praise for what our God has done. We praise Him for His Word! His mighty Word works!

However, it only works when it's put to work. Just wishing and feeling sorry for yourself won't do anything but make things worse. I know. I've tried it.

As James 1:22 says, you have to be a *doer* of the Word. James calls that Word the *"wisdom from above"* and says it is *"first pure, then peaceable, gentle, and easy to be entreated, full of mercy and good fruits, without partiality, and without hypocrisy"* (James 3:17). Let's take a close look at that description of the Word.

First—the Word is pure. It is incorruptible seed that produces the mighty supernatural crops that overwhelm the impossibilities in our lives.

Second—the Word brings peace where there is no peace.

When we began to act on the Word in Romans 4:17 by daily calling this ministry debt free, it not only looked and sounded foolish, but was hard to do. *What good is that going to do against a $5 million deficit?* I thought. But after a few days of constantly saying, "KCM is debt free in Jesus' Name," a great peace settled in me. It was like the deficit was already paid.

For many days I continued using those words to control my mind and to cast down imaginations and reasonings that exalted themselves against the Word. Every time during the day as thoughts of doubt and failure would come, I said out loud, "No you don't! I cast you down. I call this ministry debt free and every bill paid in Jesus' Name!"

I used the Word to bring my thoughts into captivity. By doing that, I was not only acting on Romans 4:17, but also 2 Corinthians 10:5.

Third—the Word is gentle. The Word and God are one. Jesus is called "the Word made flesh." The Word builds you up and makes you strong. God's Word is good.

Fourth—the Word is easy to be entreated. The Holy Spirit is here to see to it that Satan cannot stop the Word from bringing results when we entreat it. The Word is ready. The Holy Spirit is ready. He's ready when you're ready.

Fifth—the Word is full of mercy. It never leaves anyone hopeless without a way out of bondage. It is the Word of faith and hope. It is alive to bring great forgiveness and restoration to anyone who will obey and act on it.

The sixth thing is—the Word is full of good fruit. It's the seed and the seed is full. All it needs is to be planted, watered and harvested. Speaking plants it. Praise waters it, and acting as though it's already done brings in the harvest.

The seventh thing—the Word is without partiality. Anyone can put the Word to work in their lives. Absolutely anyone. The lost get saved, the sick get healed, the weak are made strong. Just like Jesus, the Word is no respecter of persons. It works when it's put to work by *anyone*.

The Word is an expression of God's love, and He so loved the world that He gave his only Son. How? The Word became flesh and dwelt among us.

Then the eighth thing—the Word is without hypocrisy. Thank God!

I wasn't a hypocrite for saying "I call this ministry debt free" before it was debt free. As long as I'm acting on the Word, I can call my body healed before the sickness leaves.

It's the Word that drives out debt. It's the Word that drives out sickness. It won't drive it out, however, unless it is believed, acted on and spoken in faith.

Faith says, "It's mine. I have it now." On what authority? Because I feel like it? No. Because it looks like it? No. Why then? Because God's Word has already said it, and I have put His Word in my mouth and have spoken His words in agreement with Him Who first spoke them.

The other thing we did to act on the Word and defeat that deficit was to keep our giving our first priority. I know, it always looks like giving is out of place when the past-due bills are piling up. But that's never the time to start holding back from God's work or from places He directs us to give. That's the time to commit yourself even deeper and closer to God to do whatever He says.

We kept our giving in place even if it meant there would be nothing left to pay the bills. Of course, as long as we kept that attitude, there was always something happening to take care of those bills.

Now that Kenneth Copeland Ministries is debt free, we are continuing to call this ministry debt free every day so that we'll never have a deficit again. The Word sets us free and the Word will keep us free.

What's more, all of us here at KCM have a great resolve to see our Partners debt free. We are calling you free from debt and lack. We consider praying and believing God for you to be free of the pressures of debt and lack just as important as praying over our own. We are one in Christ Jesus.

Go back over those eight things from James 3:17 and put the Word to work. If you're already doing that, go back over them carefully and see to it that you have not let anything slip. Touch all the bases.

Remember, we're in agreement with you for great and mighty things to happen in your life. Rise up and shout! We're free in Jesus' Name! We love you and pray for you every day.

Love,
Kenneth

September 1991

A Step of Faith Is a Step Toward Victory!

Dear Partner,

With God's grace, His favor, His honor and His face turned toward you, you can accomplish anything. All you have to do is take the next step. You don't have to do it all at once, just take the next step.

A man said to me once, "Your destination is a thousand miles from here. Each mile is connected to the other, end on end, and you have to travel them one at a time." There's no other way to get anyplace except one mile at a time. You don't have to go a thousand miles, you only have to go one mile...then another...and another until with God's power you look up and realize you have arrived.

After that, there will be another step to take, placed before you by the Holy Spirit. Another journey of faith, another adventure—but always one step at a time. That's the only way you can follow anyone, one step at a time. And Psalm 37:23 says, *"The steps of a good man are ordered by the Lord."*

God is not holding you responsible for step three or four or five, just the next step—the step of faith. He's not holding you responsible for the success of the journey. He will take care of that. You are responsible for taking the next step by faith, for being obedient to His Word and to the leading of His Spirit. The Word says obedience is greater than sacrifice.

The next step may seem like it's so insignificant that it couldn't count for much. It may be, at the moment, all you can do is something small. Don't let that keep you from taking the step. To refuse to step out because your offering is small or because whatever step you take looks insignificant compared to the problems you're facing is an act of defeat instead of an act of faith. Remember, Jesus said in Mark 4:30-32:

> **[30]Whereunto shall we liken the kingdom of God? or with what comparison shall we compare it?**
> **[31]It is like a grain of mustard seed, which, when it is sown in the earth, is less than all the seeds that be in the earth:**
> **[32]But when it is sown, it groweth up, and becometh greater than all herbs, and shooteth out great branches; so that the fowls of the air may lodge under the shadow of it.**

To refuse to plant is to refuse growth. Seeds grow when they are planted, watered and cared for.

Your next step may be to stand. Ephesians 6:13-14 says, *"...having done all, to stand. Stand therefore...."*

If you can't tell what the next step in your situation is, take the step of taking your stand on God's Word and don't be moved. Then every day read over those promises you're standing on and praise God until He shows you the next step to take.

If you say, "Brother Copeland, I don't know what promises from the Bible to stand on," then you have just identified your next step. Start reading the New Testament until you locate your situation and the promises of God that cover it. Don't try to take some other step until you take that one. No one can believe God without first hearing by the Word of God.

Look at 2 Peter 1:3-4:

³According as his divine power [God] hath given unto us all things that pertain unto life and godliness, through the knowledge of him that hath called us to glory and virtue:
⁴Whereby are given unto us exceeding great and precious promises: that by these ye might be partakers of the divine nature, having escaped the corruption that is in the world through lust.

God's Word covers every possible situation in life. It is the source of divine life and power with which we overcome the ungodly things that the storms of life throw at us.

One step of faith you can always take is praise. You can always praise God regardless of the situation, whether you feel like it or not. Praise is in the perfect will of God at any time, regardless how far out of the will of God things may look at the moment. Praise is always an act of faith, particularly when it's accompanied with the step of taking your stand.

Another step that can always be taken in any situation is giving. Even when it looks as if there's nothing to give, take the step and give anyway. Money is not the only thing available for giving. Look around you. Clean out the closets. If there's nothing left, then give of yourself. Go find someone and pray for them. There are a lot of people these days for whom just a warm heartfelt smile would be a wonderful gift.

Get involved with getting the gospel out to the world. Busy your hands and feet if you don't have anything else to give. However, don't make it some kind of religious work, make it an act of faith. Believe that every smile given is a seed planted and expect the harvest to come. As you sow that seed, do it as a step—a step toward God, a step toward victory, a step of faith and also a step on Satan's neck!

No matter how big a task you are facing today, no matter how overwhelming your situation might seem, remember: *all you have to do is take the next step.* So, stand up, look up and step out. God's Word will be there to hold you up!

Gloria and I love you and pray for you every day.

Love,
Ken

October 1990

Let Not Your Heart Be Troubled

Dear Partner,

As I write this letter, our country has just begun sending troops into the Persian Gulf. I know many believers must be wondering, *What on earth is going on?* Just as a mighty outpouring of the Holy Spirit begins, our nation is forced to go to war. Is it a coincidence? No!

God's very best is His outpouring of mighty power to save, heal, deliver and set men free. We call it revival. Satan's best (or worst) is an outpouring of destruction, disease and death. We call that war. Wars and rumors of wars have paralleled revival all down through the years, especially in the 20th century.

This has been the century of the greatest outpourings from God, and at the same time, the 20th century has seen mankind's greatest wars.

What are we supposed to do when things like this happen? Do we just pray, *"God help us,"* then hope somehow for the best?

Well, we do pray for God to help us, but there's more to it than that. The Word of God is very specific about our role of faith. And as always, we must do our part and believe God for His part.

First of all, we must settle in our own hearts that the victory is ours and the battle is the Lord's. We must rule out all possibilities of defeat—not only as individuals, but as a nation.

The next very important fact we must remind ourselves of is that there are two battles. The first one is in the heavenlies with evil and wicked spirits. The second, if it comes to it, is in the earth—man against man.

The heavenly battlefront is maintained through prayers, intercessions, giving of thanks or praising God for kings and for all who are in authority—that includes for the bad guys as well as the good. As we pray these prayers, we pull down Satan's strongholds with the Name of Jesus and the power of God's Word. According to 1 Timothy 2:1-3, such praying should be done as first priority—daily. Then, and only then, can the Church live in peace, godliness and honesty.

Now, what about when war comes? What about the times our loved ones are called into duty? Does the Word make clear what our faith part is in that case? Yes, it does.

Let's look at Matthew 24:6: *"And ye shall hear of wars and rumours of wars: see that ye be not troubled: for all these things must come to pass, but the end is not yet."*

Jesus said when we hear of wars and rumors of wars, we are not to let our hearts be troubled. A troubled or worried and upset heart is not a heart of faith. We absolutely must never turn loose of our faith. The very lives of our families and brothers and sisters in Christ Jesus depend on our faith staying strong.

I know at first that sounds like a hard thing to do at a time when war and death are at hand, but we can do it, or Jesus would not have commanded it. Since He commanded, *"Let not your heart be troubled,"* He is responsible for providing the way and the power for us to keep that command.

The first clue He gives us about how to do it is in Matthew 24:4: *"Take heed that no man deceive you."* That includes the news media—not that they are trying to deceive, but they are looking through the eyes of the world.

If we're to remain strong in faith during times of trouble, we must look not at those things or circumstances which are temporary, but at things which are eternal. We must see to it that we guard our eyes by looking at the Word—looking through God's eyes—in order not to worry and lose hope. Satan will use rumors of war to try to break down our faith and resolve even when there is no war.

Psalm 112:6-8 says that the man who delights greatly in the Word cannot be moved forever.

> [6]**Surely he shall not be moved for ever: the righteous shall be in everlasting remembrance.**
> [7]**He shall not be afraid of evil tidings: his heart is fixed, trusting in the Lord.**
> [8]**His heart is established, he shall not be afraid, until he see his desire upon his enemies.**

This man's heart is fixed. On what? On what he has established in his heart from the Word—the base, or foundation, of his trust.

The only way you can get your heart that firmly established is to look at God's promises every day and dwell on what He has said instead of what everyone around you is saying. Even if it means completely turning off the TV news and all the rest of the world's voices and locking totally into the Word until the job is done.

Finally, to be strong in the Lord means we must pay no attention to all that's being said about our enemies. Our fight of faith is not with flesh and blood. That's a particularly difficult thing to remember when, as in wartime, someone is threatening to kill us. It's a spiritual tightrope. It has to be carefully and diligently handled.

Don't enter into bad-mouthing the dictators or leaders of the enemy forces. If we are fired upon, then we must do what has to be done, but at the same time, we must refuse to hate and damn anyone. To do so will cripple our faith and that must not happen! Without faith the rest of our armor is in grave danger (Ephesians 6:16).

In closing, I want to share with you Psalm 91. I have added it to my daily prayer for you and all our Partners.

> [1] **He that dwelleth in the secret place of the most High shall abide under the shadow of the Almighty.**
> [2] **I will say of the Lord, He is my refuge and my fortress: my God; in him will I trust.**
> [3] **Surely he shall deliver thee from the snare of the fowler, and from the noisome pestilence.**
> [4] **He shall cover thee with his feathers, and under his wings shalt thou trust: his truth shall be thy shield and buckler.**
> [5] **Thou shalt not be afraid for the terror by night; nor for the arrow that flieth by day;**

[6]Nor for the pestilence that walketh in darkness; nor for the destruction that wasteth at noonday.

[7]A thousand shall fall at thy side, and ten thousand at thy right hand; but it shall not come nigh thee.

[8]Only with thine eyes shalt thou behold and see the reward of the wicked.

[9]Because thou hast made the Lord, which is my refuge, even the most High, thy habitation;

[10]There shall no evil befall thee, neither shall any plague come nigh thy dwelling.

[11]For he shall give his angels charge over thee, to keep thee in *all* thy ways.

[12]They shall bear thee up in their hands, lest thou dash thy foot against a stone.

[13]Thou shalt tread upon the lion and adder: the young lion and the dragon shalt thou trample under feet.

[14]Because he hath set his love upon me, therefore will I deliver him: I will set him on high, because he hath known my name.

[15]He shall call upon me, and I will answer him: I will be with him in trouble; I will deliver him, and honour him.

[16]With long life will I satisfy him, and show him my salvation.

Remember, this psalm was written by someone who had been in many mighty battles and had seen firsthand the salvation of God. The key words in it are *"I will say of the Lord"* and *"He will deliver me."* The truth in this psalm is what we must continue to look at and speak out. We must fix our hearts and minds not on what someone else said, but always and only on what God has said. Every time fear or doubt enters your mind, say this out loud:

> I dwell in the secret place of the most High and under the shadow of the Almighty. I say of the Lord, He is my refuge and my fortress. He is my God! I trust Him! My heart is fixed forever. Even when everyone is shouting shortage, I am shouting, "He delivers me from the snare of the fowler and all his noise! I refuse to fear. I trust Him!"

In fact, do it right now—go through that whole psalm along with Psalm 112:6-8. Say it out loud. Say it louder than the TV news. That's important.

Wow! Just writing this letter has stirred my spirit.

Well, must close. Gloria and I love you and pray for you every day.

Love,
Kenneth

December 1990

Jesus—Your Brother, Your Friend

Dear Partner,

Have you ever heard someone refer to Jesus as the "only begotten Son of God"? It's a common expression based on 1 John 4:9 which says, *"God sent his only begotten Son into the world."*

Certainly, Jesus was God's only begotten Son when He first sent Him into the world. But He is no longer the *only begotten*. Romans 8:29 says the reason Jesus came into this world was so He could become the *firstborn of many brethren*. Hebrews 2:11 says *He's not ashamed to call us His brethren.*

Jesus is your big Brother! Think about that!

I know that kind of talk upsets some religious folks. But being reborn with God as your Father and Jesus as your very own Brother is what the good news is all about.

Not only that, Jesus is also our Lord—Conqueror of death and hell, Overcomer of the world and the flesh. He did it and He did it all for you and me!

If that was all, it would be more than enough, but that's not all He did. He also accepted God's appointment as High Priest of our profession (the words of our mouths). He then authorized us to speak His Words by giving exceeding great and precious promises that cover every aspect of our lives, both in heaven and in earth. As we believe and speak those promises, the very throne of His grace is the guarantee that what we say will come to pass.

In addition to all that, He gave us His Name, the Name which is above all names. The Name which has been given all authority has been given to you and me to use in faith and declare our redemption from the curse. Oh thank God, heaven comes to attention and hell trembles when we speak in that Name.

Jesus came to this Earth to bring to us all of these mighty things, but again, that's not all. He also came to be a good friend. He's not a condemning friend. He's never a tattletale or a backstabber. He's the One Who is always on your side— all the time. He's Someone to talk to and Someone to listen to. He loves you more than you know.

He not only gave Himself for us at Calvary, He gave Himself for us and to us forever. He's talking about you right now. He even makes intercession for you and me.

Take some time right now and tell Jesus how much you love and appreciate Him. Tell the Father how grateful you are to Him for sending Jesus to you and redeeming your life. Be still for a few minutes each day during this busy time of year and bless the Lord, ministering to Him in praise from your innermost being. Think and talk about these things.

Before I close, I want to thank you for your prayers for this ministry and for Gloria and me. What a joy it is to realize that my Partners are always praying and standing with us. Gloria and I love you very much and we pray for you every day.

Love,
Kenneth

January 1991

Declare Victory Over Debt

Dear Partner,

Let's go for it! A debt-free lifestyle now!

The Lord has directed KCM to launch an all-out Victory Campaign against debt, poverty and lack in the Body of Christ. It's time to shake off the shackles that have bound us in the past and come to the place where the Holy Spirit has command over our financial lives instead of the debtors and doubters.

The thing I hear ringing in my spirit loud and clear is not only to get out of debt, but stay out.

Now that doesn't mean we'll never have anything. No! It means, thank God, by His grace we'll be all sufficient in all things (2 Corinthians 9:8).

I want to share some principles with you from God's Word that will help clear up your thinking and renew your mind concerning heaven's plan to supply God's people.

He never intended for the Body of Christ to be bound to the world and its financial ups and downs. He never intended for us to look to the world to meet our needs. He intended for the world to come to Jesus through *us* to get *their* needs met, instead of our going to them with our hat in our hand, bowing before them to borrow according to their terms. He said in Deuteronomy 28:12-13:

¹²The Lord shall open unto thee his good treasure, the heaven to give the rain unto thy land in his season, and to bless all the work of thine hand: and thou shalt lend unto many nations, and thou shalt not borrow.

¹³And the Lord shall make thee the head, and not the tail; and thou shalt be above only, and thou shalt not be beneath; if that thou hearken unto the commandments of the Lord thy God, which I command thee this day, to observe and to do them.

God's way is for us to look to Jesus, the Head of the Church, for our supply. To do that we must turn to His Word, find out His ways and then walk in them.

Gloria and I have been endeavoring to walk in the Word concerning our finances since 1967. We've seen some rough and tough times as you know, but we've also seen the glory of the Lord and experienced His salvation. We've been debt free for over 20 years by looking to the Word instead of leaning to our own understanding.

But our understanding had to change before we could live that way. We couldn't look to the world to tell us how to receive from heaven—they don't know how. Sadly enough, we couldn't look to most Christians—they didn't know how either, and in some cases, they actually resisted the whole idea. We had to turn to the Word and stay on it. Thank God, it worked and it's still working.

If you want to live debt free, one of the first things you

must know is that prosperity, or increase, is produced by the Word—not the world. The law of increase Jesus taught about in Mark 4:21-32 does not depend on a race or any certain set of circumstances. It doesn't depend on a form of government or the availability of material goods. The law of increase is based on the Word. It works anywhere any time it is put to work by faith by anyone who will believe it and walk in it.

Think about this. Do we only preach salvation to people who are saved? Certainly not. The Word *brings* salvation. Do we only preach healing where there are no sick? No, the Word *brings* healing. Well, by the same token, we don't just preach prosperity where there is money. The Word brings increase anywhere it is preached. *Anywhere!*

The kingdom of God is our home. It is our source of supply. Jesus said to seek it first and all things would be added to us. (See Matthew 6:33.)

Make the decision today to be free. The very first step toward that freedom is a step of faith. Lay your hands over your own heart and say before the Lord, *"I receive You, Jesus, as Lord over my finances. I look to You for my deliverance from debt and lack."*

Now read Philippians 4 out loud before Jesus, the High Priest of your confession, and claim *every* word with all your heart. You have a right to every word because Paul wrote it to his partners and I'm writing it to my Partner—you! We are in this together to get God's Word out to the nations.

There's power in the Word of God! There's power in agreement! So when we agree with you that you're delivered from debt and lack in Jesus' Name—great power is going to be released.

Right now, say, "Thank God, I'm debt free and will stay debt free. That's my lifestyle. More than enough. More than enough through Jesus Who meets *all* my needs according to His riches in glory."

Declare victory over debt today!

Love,
Kenneth

February 1991

Stretch Your Faith

Dear Partner,

What a time for God's people to excel in faith, hope and love! We have the greater opportunity to live victoriously on this Earth than any generation since Jesus was resurrected and seated at the right hand of glory.

There's never been a greater time to push our faith. No matter how strong your faith is, begin to push it and put pressure on it to enlarge its capacity. Remember, it's God's faith that dwells in you and Jesus is the developer of it. It will grow if you feed it and exercise it.

Too much of the time we've all been too quick to settle for "good enough" instead of God's best. That's especially true where our finances are concerned.

The devil would like nothing better than to keep us bound down to debt, lack, poverty and financial weakness in order to keep us under the thumb of the world's ungodly way of doing things. He'd like nothing better than to render us impotent and without influence in world affairs. Not to mention cutting us short and preventing us from getting God's Word out to the sick and dying masses of people that need Jesus so badly!

Here we are, the generation that has been given more equipment both in technology and spiritual revelation

STRETCH YOUR FAITH | 161

with which to reach mankind, and we've been so bogged down in debt and lack, we haven't been doing what we should have.

Think about this. Even in our bound and bogged-down condition, the Body of Christ has still affected the whole world with the gospel of Jesus. Think about what is about to happen as more and more of God's people are set free to give and to go—by the millions. Wow!

Now let me share with you what I mean by stretching and developing your faith. Look at your own situation and surroundings and decide what the next step up should be. Where *should* you be in your giving? Where *should* you be in your income? If you are ministering, where *should* your ministry be? What's the next step toward *what should be?*

Now go to the Word and believe Philippians 4:13—you can do all things through God's Anointed One which strengthens you. Begin to think of yourself that way: free in Jesus, doing God's best instead of being satisfied, or worse yet, just putting up with things the way they are.

Believe me, things will either get better by faith and grow or they'll get worse. They won't just stay the same.

Sometimes the very mention of living debt free sets off a storm of unbelief. I was praying about this last week and the Lord said, "When people ask, 'Brother Copeland, how could we ever build a new church without borrowing the money? It's *so* much.' Tell them if you don't have the faith to build the church without going in debt, you won't have the faith to make the payments."

It takes the same faith to believe God for cash up front as it does to believe Him for 30 or 40 years of big payments and all that interest that's going into the world's pockets. The same would be true of a home or any other project that's dedicated to God and to your welfare.

Now that's what I mean by stretching your faith. Don't build a church or a house or whatever before you spend enough time meditating in God's Word to know in your heart you really can do all things with Jesus strengthening you. During that meditation and faith-stretching time in the Word, you will hear from God. He'll show you what to do. He'll show you how to do it. He'll show you when to do it. And He'll finance you.

You belong to Him. It gives Him great pleasure to prosper you, especially when you go to Him instead of the world to get your needs met.

As always and in everything, the Word of God is the key. It must come first. The bigger the problem or the bigger the project, the more the Word should be your first concern, and it (the Word of God) should get all your attention—not the other way around.

Don't give your attention to the size of the problem. Give your attention to the Word. Then the problem will begin to lose its formidability. It will begin to shrink and you'll laugh and say, "My God meets my needs according to His riches in glory." That's when you're ready to go ahead with the project and not until.

Gloria and I have lived this way since 1967, and I can tell you the Word works! Put it to work!

Love,
Kenneth

March 1991

Victory, Brother!

Dear Partner,

Right now all over this nation and the world, battles are going on—military battles, political battles, economic battles. Conditions are so intense that it's tempting to listen constantly to the media for the latest news and information.

But the Lord reminded me again last night—the most important thing in our victory is our *faith*. Faith doesn't come by hearing the TV news. Faith comes by hearing and hearing by the Word of God.

Wars are won and lost first on the spiritual field of battle and then on the earthly battlefields—not the other way around. We must keep our faith strong at all times, and sometimes that means turning off the TV and radio and putting a tape in the tape player, a tape that shouts victory in Jesus. After all, that's where the real victory lies.

I want you to know, we haven't let up on our campaign to break the power of debt, lack and poverty in your life and ministry and in the Body of Christ. We haven't let up on the devil one bit.

In fact, we've come down on him even harder with an even greater resolve to do the mighty works of Jesus in spite of anything Satan cooks up. We serve The Mighty God—Possessor of heaven and Earth. If He's for us, who then can be against us? We are more than conquerors in Christ Jesus.

Wars, rumors of wars and other threatening circumstances don't change a thing in the Great Commission. Our primary calling from Jesus to every believer is still to *go into all the world and preach the gospel to every creature with signs following.*

Jesus said in Matthew 24:14, this gospel will be preached to all the world as a witness to all nations and then the end shall come. A witness is evidence or signs following.

Even in the midst of deadly, trying, and in some cases, tragic times, our mission and calling does not change. We must keep our eyes on that mission and on the One Who called us—Jesus of Nazareth, King of kings. He's the only One in all this Who really knows what He's doing. We must not ever turn loose of that fact regardless of how circumstances around us may look.

Gloria and I have renewed our commitment to our Most High Commander, Jesus, to put His Word out to this war-torn, sin-racked world in every place and in every way He directs. I want you to know you are Partners with a ministry that does not draw back from danger. Whatever Jesus says for us to say, we will say it. What He says to do, we will do. And we'll do it all in His strength and power.

In closing this letter today, I encourage you to put victory in Jesus on your lips. Say it out loud to every believer you meet—"Victory, Brother. Victory in Jesus!"

Jesus is coming!

Victory, Brother!
JESUS IS LORD!
Kenneth

April 1991

Keep the Faith-Pressure On

Dear Partner,

I want to begin this letter by expressing the love that the Lord Jesus has placed in Gloria's and my heart for you. It is really amazing how it continues to grow inside us, especially as we make mention of you every day in our prayers.

You and all of our other Partners are at the very center of this ministry. We're reaching out with God's Word to the world with all our might, but our love and faith "target" is always our Partners. You are ever on our hearts and in our prayers.

As you know, this ministry has been engaged in an all-out, maximum-effort campaign against debt, poverty and lack.

Recently, someone asked me, "How goes the war on debt?"

"What war?" I answered. "The war's been won by our Champion, Jesus! We are just exercising our victory rights and weapons in Him."

I am thrilled to tell you that victory reports and testimonies are flooding this office. Every kind of miracle you can think of has been reported, plus a few we had never thought of before. Supernatural, outright miracles of God's glory are destroying debts and opening up doors of opportunity and blessings.

So keep the faith-pressure on!

1. **Keep your faith fed on the Word.** Your faith is working. Whether you've seen any results or not doesn't matter. The Word works as long as you keep your faith vibrant and alive to the victory. Remember, breakthroughs happen in the unseen world before they take place in the seen world.

2. **Keep your confession bold and filled with praise.** We really don't have any idea how terrible our faith-filled words of victory are on the ears of darkness and the spirits of poverty and lack. They cannot stand against the pressure of it. It's just too much for them. They must let go of what belongs to you in Jesus. They must flee!

   So don't let up. Rejoice continually—whether you feel like it or not and whether it looks like it's working or not. The Word says it is working, so it is!

3. **Keep giving.** Search for ways to give. Give your money. Give of your things. Most of all, give of yourself. If you wind up without any money, sell something and give. Search out your house for things you can give. Don't just give old discarded things, give of the good stuff, too. Give—not until it hurts—but until it gets so good you can't stop. When there's no more stuff to give, remind the Lord, *"It's time for more stuff so I can keep on giving."*

4. **Seek the kingdom.** Spend time giving yourself to God. Spend quality time studying and meditating God's Word. It's good to listen to tapes on the way to

work and so forth, but we all need some real giving of our time—our most valuable asset—to Jesus and the Holy Spirit. Jesus said if we would do that, all these *things* would be added to us.

Giving is a release of the *agape* love of God that has been shed abroad in our hearts by the Holy Spirit. It is powerful! It is overwhelming to the works of the devil. It will completely drive from your life the forces of doubt, unbelief, poverty, debt, sin, sickness, demons, fear or anything else hell has to offer. It is the very life of God Himself.

He so *loved* the world that He *gave* Jesus, His very best. However, that was not the end of it. He began receiving many sons and daughters, including the return of Jesus—this original gift—to His right side forever. He's been receiving ever since in a steady stream, sons and daughters.

He also just keeps on giving, loving, blessing, caring, healing, delivering, pouring out of Himself upon all flesh who will receive. Hallelujah!

As you give to God, do it with a joyous heart. Victory in Jesus is all around us. Lay your hand on every offering and bless it and command it, saying, "Go, seed of faith. Reach the lost. Bring faith to God's people and joy to the heart of my heavenly Father."

Then praise Jesus' Name, saying, "Come miracles. Come riches in God's glory. Go lack. Go poverty. Go debt. I'm free. Free in Jesus' Name!"

Victory, Brother! Victory in Jesus! Jesus is Lord!

Love,
Ken

May 1991

New Life—Now!

Dear Partner,

Praise God, it's springtime! Things are budding out with new life and as I watch them, I can't help but think about the new life that Jesus put in us when we were born again.

You know, if we continually feed our inner man on God's Word, that budding, flowing wellspring of God's life is fresh every day. Second Corinthians 4:16 says it this way, *"For which cause we faint not; but though our outward man perish, yet the inward man is renewed day by day."*

Read the entire 4th chapter of 2 Corinthians and you'll see that the phrase, *"though the outward man is perishing,"* is not referring, in this case, to aging. Of course, it's true that the body is aging, but here the Apostle Paul is talking about all the afflictions and persecutions the devil used to try to destroy his life and ministry. (He lists them in verses 8-11.)

I like to say verse 16 like this, "Therefore, I don't get discouraged. Even though I get beaten on the outside, my inner man is budding with new life every day."

New life! The eternal, unquenchable life of Almighty God. That life is in you, now! It doesn't need to come down from heaven again—it's already here. It's inside you. God's Word calls it a heavenly treasure inside earthly bodies (2 Corinthians 4:7). It just needs to be fed and stirred up on

God's Word—regularly—just as your body needs food on a regular basis. Jesus said we don't live by bread alone but by or on every word that God says.

Romans 6:4 tells us that *"as Christ was raised up from the dead by the glory of the Father, even so we also should walk in newness of life."*

Think about that! Walking in newness of life! The term "walking in" means living in it constantly, every day, all the time, all our life.

We should wake up every morning in a new victory. Wake up with victory in Jesus on our minds regardless of what's going on in our bodies and regardless of what is happening around us. Your first thought every day should be that Jesus has been raised from the dead and His victory is your victory.

It doesn't matter how hard things around you have become—you're still bigger on the inside than you are on the outside. The Greater One lives in you. His life is in you—now!

I didn't say it was easy to think and speak and act in newness of life at all times. If it was, everyone would be doing it. I am saying you can do it by faith.

All that junk Satan throws at you and me, trying to destroy our walk with Jesus, can be tough. But it can never overthrow the newness of life dwelling inside you. That life is just chomping at the bit to get released into the face of the enemy in order to bring great victory over his works of darkness.

It is ready to drive poverty, lack, debt, sickness, grief, doubt, unbelief and any other wicked work from you. And it will keep you free! Free! Free in Jesus! If your mind is giving you a hard time about thinking thoughts of victory, just shout out loud:

> *I'm free in Jesus, mind! You'll think the way I tell you to think! I am the saved. I am the healed. I am the prosperous. I am free from debt. I am in Jesus and His life is in me.*

Then shout to the devil:

> *I am free, Devil. You understand that? In Jesus' Name I am free. Take your hands off my mind. Take your hands off my body. Take your hands off my money. You're not my god. Jesus is my Lord. And I'm free. Victory is mine.*

When you shout those things, something happens inside your spirit—your inner man. Life begins to flow—God's life. The Word of God that you've been studying and feeding on leaps into your mouth and gets your "newness of life walk" going in the right direction.

Of course, it will work whether you shout it or whether you just say it. The very act of speaking it out has an effect on your mind because your mind has to stop and see what your mouth has to say. But there are times when it does you good to shout your faith.

Speak these same words of victory when you give offerings and when you tithe your tithe. Regardless of what ministry your offering is going into, release life from deep inside your being before you release the offering. Sow your seeds of faith and love with words of victory in praise.

You are redeemed, so say so. Do it right now. Lay hands on this letter and *say so!* Declare your redemption!!

May God's very best flow like a flood to you and over all your hand touches. We love you and pray for you every day.

Love,
Kenneth

June 1991

You're a Child of the King

Dear Partner,

God is moving all over the Earth. Stay with Him. Stay in the Word. Every day read and meditate something from God's Word about our redemption and sonship in Jesus.

God has delivered us from the authority of darkness and has translated us into the kingdom of the dear Son of His love in Whom we have redemption through His blood (Colossians 1:13-14).

Begin to think about that all day instead of all the problems and cares of this world that are surrounding you. Jesus said the cares of this world *entering* in will choke the Word. Don't let them enter.

It's not your business to try to figure out all that stuff anyway. It's your and my business to keep the Word of our redemption hot and alive in our spirits and minds. It's God's business to meet our needs according to His riches in glory.

Look at Colossians 2:9-10: *"For in him dwelleth all the fulness of the Godhead bodily. And ye are complete in him, which is the head of all principality and power."* Does that sound like a description of some pitiful, poor weakling that can barely make ends meet? No! It's a description of the child of the King.

Read on—verses 12-15:

[12]Buried with him in baptism, wherein also ye are risen with him through the faith of the operation of God, who hath raised him from the dead.

[13]And you, being dead in your sins and the uncircumcision of your flesh, hath he quickened together with him, having forgiven you all trespasses;

[14]Blotting out the handwriting of ordinances that was against us, which was contrary to us, and took it out of the way, nailing it to his cross;

[15]And having spoiled principalities and powers, he made a show of them openly, triumphing over them in it.

Look at that! Jesus whipped the devil and his whole crowd just for you. He defeated him, and then He gave us the keys to the ball and chain that He put around Satan's neck.

He gave us His very own Name. The Name of Jesus! Say that Name right now, out loud.

JESUS!

Acts 10:38 says, *"God anointed Jesus of Nazareth with the Holy Ghost and with power: who went about doing good, and healing all that were oppressed of the devil; for God was with him."* Jesus is still anointed. God is still with Him. His Name is as anointed as He is. Philippians 2:9-11 says:

[9]Wherefore God also hath highly exalted him, and given him a name which is *above every name:*

[10]That at the name of Jesus every knee should bow, of things in heaven, and things in earth, and things under the earth;

[11]And that every tongue should confess that Jesus Christ is Lord, to the glory of God the Father.

Say that Name *out loud* again.

JESUS!

Let the sound of it ring in your spirit. Listen to it in a fresh, new, faith-filled way. JESUS!

Now say this along with me (I'm saying this out loud while I'm writing this):

Satan, take your hands off all that's mine. You are forever defeated and I am forever redeemed. In the Name of Jesus, I am free from your bondage. Jesus is my Lord and Him I will serve forever.

Keep that thought on your mind. Crowd out everything else by saying it out loud. That's very important. Take the thought by saying it. Stay with it. It will explode in a breakthrough for you that you'll never forget—and neither will the devil.

Gloria and I love you with all our hearts.

Love,
Kenneth

July 1991

No Weapon Formed Against You Shall Prosper!

Dear Partner,

In Philippians 1:19-20 the Apostle Paul wrote to his partners, *"For I know that this shall turn to my salvation through your prayer, and the supply of the Spirit of Jesus Christ, According to my earnest expectation...."*

Paul knew that his life was being sustained by the Holy Spirit through the prayers of his partners. He earnestly expected the prayers of his partners to be answered.

More and more every day that goes by, I realize that Gloria's and my life and ministry are being sustained in the power of the Holy Ghost through the prayers of my Partners. That realization has grown inside me over the years until it's as though my Partners are with me and never leave me, day in and day out.

My thoughts are wrapped up in ministering to you on TV, on tape, in books, in meetings, or any other way God leads us to get the message of God's Word to you. You are the first objective in this ministry. Seeing you grow and prosper in the Lord Jesus is our greatest blessing because we have you in our hearts.

In this letter I want to share with you a scripture I have added to the scriptures that we already pray for you every day. It is a scripture that I have stood on in my own personal life more than any other, and it has brought many great victories to me and to my family. It is found in Isaiah 54:8-17:

[8]In a little wrath I hid my face from thee for a moment; but with everlasting kindness will I have mercy on thee, saith the Lord thy Redeemer.

[9]For this is as the waters of Noah unto me: for as I have sworn that the waters of Noah should no more go over the earth; so have I sworn that I would not be wroth with thee, nor rebuke thee.

[10]For the mountains shall depart, and the hills be removed; but my kindness shall not depart from thee, neither shall the covenant of my peace be removed, saith the Lord that hath mercy on thee.

[11]O thou afflicted, tossed with tempest, and not comforted, behold, I will lay thy stones with fair colours, and lay thy foundations with sapphires.

[12]And I will make thy windows of agates, and thy gates of carbuncles, and all thy borders of pleasant stones.

[13]And all thy children shall be taught of the Lord; and great shall be the peace of thy children.

[14]In righteousness shalt thou be established: thou shalt be far from oppression; for thou shalt not fear: and from terror; for it shall not come near thee.

¹⁵**Behold, they shall surely gather together, but not by me: whosoever shall gather together against thee shall fall for thy sake.**

These next two verses contain one of the greatest promises in the Bible. In them, God takes the responsibility for *creating* Satan and for *defeating* him.

¹⁶**Behold, I have created the smith that bloweth the coals in the fire, and that bringeth forth an instrument for his work; and I have created the waster to destroy.**
¹⁷**No weapon that is formed against thee shall prosper; and every tongue that shall rise against thee in judgment thou shalt condemn. This is the heritage of the servants of the Lord, and their righteousness is of me, saith the Lord.**

Notice Who is speaking in that passage—*"The Lord thy Redeemer"* (verse 8). The chapter just before this one (Isaiah 53) speaks of Jesus' crucifixion. Then here in Chapter 58, He is shown raised from the dead and glorified as our Redeemer. What's the first thing God says to us after Jesus is glorified? You can find it in verse 9. *"In the same way I swore that I would never flood the earth again, I promise I will never again be wroth with you nor rebuke you."*

Praise God, that's where our prayer promise begins! Let me show you how to pray it for yourself. Start with verses 10-12:

*I thank you, Lord, that Your kindness and the
covenant of Your peace shall never depart from me.
Thank You that You have laid my stones with fair
colors and my foundations with sapphires, my windows with agates, and my gates with carbuncles,
and all my borders with pleasant stones.*

You see, God looks at us not only as His children, but as
kings and priests (Revelation 1:6). In His eyes, nothing is too
good for us. He sees us in Jesus.

*Thank You Lord, that all my children are taught
of the Lord, and great is the peace of my children
(verse 13).*

I pray this not only for my own children and grandchil-
dren, but also for my spiritual children.

*Thank You, Lord, that I am established in Your
righteousness. Jesus said to seek first Your kingdom
and Your righteousness and all these things would
be added unto me. I receive it done.*

*Thank God, fear, oppression, and terror are not
from God. If they're not from God, I'll not receive
them! They shall fall for my sake. Fall, fear! Fall,
oppression! Fall, terror! You're not from God, and
you'll not come near me (verse 14).*

*I thank You, Jesus, that You have defeated
the devil and all his words. No weapon formed
against me shall prosper and every tongue that rises*

against me shall be condemned or brought to nothing. This is my inheritance and my blood-bought right in Jesus. The Lord says so! (verses 16-17).

Look how that ends: *"The Lord says so."* In these verses, God is saying, "All of this is theirs because I say it is." The devil has no say in this matter.

Right now, go down through these verses, pray them and receive every promise. Pray them out loud and then let the Lord speak to you after each verse. Think about what each one is saying. Think about who you are in Christ Jesus.

After you've believed you receive, go back over them again and pray them for Gloria and me and for this ministry. My earnest expectation is already jumping up and down inside me. Just think about all of us Covenant Partners praying this for one another literally all over the world. Hell is weeping in its defeat. Its ears are ringing with, *"Their righteousness is of me, saith the Lord!"*

As I said, I'm adding this to the prayer scripture list that I pray for you every day. Please add it to yours.

Until I write again, remember: Faith works! Love works! The Word works!

Love,
Kenneth

August 1991

Just Do It!

Dear Partner,

The outpouring we've been looking for and hearing the Lord prophesy about for years has really started! Recently Gloria and I attended a meeting where there was a healing explosion just like those back in the tent days of the '50s. Brother Oral Roberts was so excited about it that he was "shouting happy" the whole time we were there.

Remember the prophecy I wrote you about? The one in which the Lord spoke and said that the Berlin Wall was coming down? In that message He said when it came down it would be a sign that the outpouring had begun. Well, the wall came down and the outpouring has begun with great glory.

What does that mean to people like you and me who are already living by faith and walking in God's Word?

First of all, it means this is a time to receive from God. It's a time to gather up all the loose ends in our lives and release our faith—especially in areas where results have been seemingly slow in coming. I'm talking about those aches and pains and different harassments that have hung around too long. It's time to pull those strongholds down.

It's also a time to listen more carefully to the Holy Spirit for direction and revelation. That means spending extra time in the Word and prayer, especially taking a few more minutes of quiet time each day to listen.

Another very important thing to remember during times of revival and outpouring is to keep yourself ready to be called on by the Lord to minister to others. Stay available. You'll walk away from praying for someone saying, "I've never in my life seen it so easy to pray for people."

There will be times that it will seem like everyone you touch will get healed and everyone you witness to will want to make Jesus Lord of their life.

In the midst of it all, don't neglect gathering together with other believers. Go to meetings. Have prayer meetings of your own. Don't miss church. I remember during the '60s when prayer groups were more fun than anything I had ever experienced. Well, those times are here again. Only this time it's already as strong as it was then—and it has only just begun.

I received a word from the Lord this morning while I was praying for you and the other Partners. I saw a large, safe-like box that said "FOOD BOX" in big letters on the front, just above a big handle that locked the door. Just below the handle was a sign that said, "To open, turn left and pull."

When I saw it, I knew in my spirit two things. First, it was full of everything I needed. Second, it could not be opened any other way except the way the sign said. Then the Lord spoke to me, *Why would you want to try to open that door any other way than according to the sign—turn left and pull?* He said, *Why not just do what it says?*

When the Word says, *"Hold fast to our confession,"* why

not just do it? When it says, *"Having done all to stand,"* why not just stand? When the Word says *"Think on these things"* or *"Don't be anxious about anything, but in everything in thanksgiving and prayer let your requests be made known unto God,"* why not just...turn left and pull? Do what it says, then God will do what He says!

In my mind's eye, I could just see someone standing in front of that box, trying to turn the handle to the right or trying to pull it open without turning it, all just because that's the way they *feel* like it should work. They will eventually walk away saying that the box just wasn't for them or that it was probably empty anyway.

That's the way the devil starts lies to keep people out of the box where the food is. Eventually people will be bowing down before that box, trying to worship God and never opening the box, never receiving from its bounty—even though all the time, as plain as day, on the front of that box it says "turn left and pull."

Obedience to God's Word is how the treasures of God's wisdom and knowledge are released. We walk by faith, not by sight. Just do it!

This *is* a time to receive from God. Oh my, I'm excited about it! This *is* the time for you to receive deliverance from those pains and harassments that have been hanging around you. It is time to pull those strongholds down. So turn left and pull—then get ready to receive from God!

Gloria and I love you and pray for you every day.

Love,
Kenneth

October 1991

Release Your Hope

Dear Partner,

The glory of God is falling all over the world. The reports of the Holy Spirit's mighty acts are coming in from everywhere by the stacks—more than any of us have ever seen. We are seeing the end-time drama being played out right before our very eyes.

This ministry is being given opportunities to take God's Word into places where only a short time ago it was impossible. The doors are opening and we are stepping through them as fast as we can. The things that so many have prayed for and in the past have even died for are suddenly coming to pass.

The iron is hot—let's strike!

I want to share something with you today that will help your faith. It certainly has helped mine.

All of my life I've heard people say, "I sure do hope so." I didn't pay any attention to it until I began living by faith, but then I realized how void of faith and power that phrase is. I didn't understand why it was so empty when the Bible is full of the word *hope.*

When I heard people say, "We're just hoping and praying," my spirit would withdraw. "Unbelief!" my heart would cry. Why? Is hope a bad word? Absolutely not. The problem is that most people don't really understand it.

The way we use the word hope in everyday speech and the meaning of hope as used in the Bible are two different things. When we say, "I hope so," we simply mean *I desire* or *I wish*. Bible hope isn't wishing at all. It is *earnest, confident, favorable, intense expectation*—and that's something else entirely.

Colossians 1:23 talks about *"the hope of the gospel."* Acts 26:6 uses the phrase *"hope of the promise"* referring to the covenant God made with Abraham. That kind of hope is an earnest, intense expectation that comes from God's promises. There's a vast difference between "I wish something would happen," and "I intensely expect that to happen."

In Philippians 1:19 and 20, the Apostle Paul says:

[19]**For I know that this shall turn to my salvation through your prayer, and the supply of the Spirit of Jesus Christ,**
[20]*According to my earnest expectation and my hope*, **that in nothing I shall be ashamed, but that with all boldness, as always, so now also Christ shall be magnified in my body, whether it be by life, or by death.**

Here, Paul used two Greek words together, one meaning *earnest expectation* and the other, translated *hope*, meaning the same thing. Those words can also be translated like this, "according to my earnest, confident, intense expectation."

Usually when someone is that expectant over something, everyone wants to know why—especially if that person is expecting something that looks impossible. This is where

Hebrews 11:1 comes in. Faith is the substance, the under-pinning of things hoped for. And where does faith come from? *"Faith cometh by hearing, and hearing by the word of God"* (Romans 10:17).

Even when there is no natural evidence that what I hope for will come to pass, I can be expectant because I have faith in God's word. Hope won't work without faith, and faith won't work without hope. Neither one will work without the Word.

Hope is always expectant, looking toward the future. Faith is always now! Without hope, faith has nothing to bring to pass. Without faith, tomorrow never comes. Put them together and—look out!—something wonderful takes place in the world of the spirit and then is transferred into the world of matter (this physical world where all the trouble is).

Real Bible hope rejoices. It begins to shout long before anything happens in the natural because it looks into the future and sees you whole. It sees you debt free. It sees you healed. It sees you victorious in Jesus Who is our hope (1 Timothy 1:1).

How do I get that kind of hope? First of all, remember you don't have to "get it," you only have to release it. It's already in you because Jesus is in you. Then take these four steps.

Step 1: Since hope comes from the promises, find the promises in God's Word that cover your situation.

Step 2: Lay hold upon the hope that is set before you (Hebrews 6:18). Point your finger at that Bible promise and say out loud, "I believe that. It's mine. It's talking about me."

Step 3: Think about that promise all day long. See yourself with the answer. Second Corinthians 10:3-6 says this is the way the battle is fought and won. Cast down imaginations. Bring into captivity every thought, not just a few thoughts, *every thought* that disagrees with your promise from God.

Step 4: Put the promises in your mouth all day, every day. Say your faith by saying those verses. Say them before the Lord. Say them before the devil—LOUD. Say them in your own ears—hundreds, even thousands of times. Say them until the earnest, intense, favorable, confident expectation begins to rise on the inside of you. That's hope, real Bible hope.

I expect it—
because God promised it!
I believe it's happening for me now—
because God promised it!

As far as I am concerned, it's done. Why? Because God promised it.

Before I close, I want you to lay your hands on this letter and pray with all of us here at KCM. We really have our hands full keeping up with all the Lord Jesus is calling us to do. We can do it! The greater One lives within us. We see it done!

Gloria and I love you and we pray for you every day.

Love,
Kenneth

November/December 1991

They Saw a Giant, He Saw a Prize!

Dear Partner,

A number of years ago the Lord said, "If I showed you the things I'm going to do, you wouldn't be able to believe it." Well, those times are here.

These are truly the days we've all prayed to see. A flood of the Holy Spirit is being poured out. Miracles of healing and deliverance are gushing forth in meetings everywhere, in churches, at home in front of TV sets—wherever people are talking about Jesus.

Recently, we heard a mother testify that the Lord had opened her young son's eyelid which had been closed since birth. It happened at school when two of his young classmates laid hands on him in Jesus' Name.

Aren't these things wonderful? And this is only the beginning. Just a few days ago we heard the Lord say again, "If I told you of the things I'm about to do, you couldn't believe it." I don't believe He's anywhere near through on the world scene.

When Jesus said the gospel of the kingdom would be preached to all nations as a witness and then the end would come, He meant every word of it. No religion can stop it. No government can stop it. No devil can stop it.

It's happening now right in front of our very eyes. Let's not miss a bit of it. Our God is moving! Let's get right in the middle of it.

I want to share something from the Word with you today that the Lord showed me a few days ago right in the middle of a sermon I was preaching. It was so exciting that it has been in the forefront of my mind ever since.

You can find it in 1 Samuel 17:22-27:

²²And (David) ran into the army, and came and saluted his brethren,

²³And as he talked with them, behold, there came up the champion, the Philistine of Gath, Goliath by name, out of the armies of the Philistines, and spake according to the same words: and David heard them.

²⁴And all the men of Israel, when they saw the man, fled from him, and were sore afraid.

²⁵And the men of Israel said, Have ye seen this man that is come up? surely to defy Israel is he come up: and it shall be, that the man who killeth him, the king will enrich him with great riches, and will give him his daughter, and make his father's house free in Israel.

²⁶And David spake to the men that stood by him, saying, What shall be done to the man that killeth this Philistine, and taketh away the reproach from Israel? For who is this uncircumcised Philistine, that he should defy the armies of the living God?

[27]And the people answered him after this manner, saying, So shall it be done to the man that killeth him.

If you read those verses carefully, you'll see that the statement David made in verse 26 was actually spoken *before* the Israelite men spoke the words recorded in verse 25. So, let's reverse those two verses and read them that way:

[26]And David spake to the men that stood by him, saying, What shall be done to the man that killeth this Philistine, and taketh away the reproach from Israel? For who is this uncircumcised Philistine, that he should defy the armies of the living God?

[25]And the men of Israel said, Have ye seen this man that is come up? surely to defy Israel is he come up: and it shall be, that the man who killeth him, the king will enrich him with great riches, and will give him his daughter, and make his father's house free in Israel.

[27]And the people answered him after this manner...."

For 40 days, twice a day, this giant had shouted his curses. And for 40 days the army of Israel had cowered before him in fear. Then David came along and—

INSTEAD OF SEEING A GIANT,
HE SAW AN OPPORTUNITY!

"What does the man get who kills this giant?" asked David.

"Have you seen how big he is?" answered the Israelite officers.

David wasn't worried about how big he was. In fact, in David's eyes, Goliath's size made him a more valuable prize.

The Apostle Paul had the same kind of victorious attitude. He said he gloried in tribulations. He considered them opportunities for mighty victories—opportunities to give more glory to Jesus and the power of His Word.

Like Paul, David knew the power of God's Word, and he wasn't intimidated by the lies of his enemy. When Goliath stepped out, he shouted at David, "*Am I a dog, that thou comest to me with staves?...Come to me, and I will give thy flesh unto the fowls of the air, and to the beasts of the field*" (1 Samuel 17:43-44). David didn't turn and run like everyone else had for over six weeks. He didn't see a giant. He saw a prize and *shouted back* in the name of the Lord God of Hosts!

Once David began to shout, the giant couldn't get in another word. David's words in God's name took over. That's really when he won the battle. He spoke in God's name and from that point the battle was the Lord's.

Then David did something very important. He ran toward his prize. He attacked it, knocked it down, stood on it and cut off its head. He wasn't about to let it get up again—ever!

In Mark 11:23 Jesus essentially told us to do the same thing. He said, *Speak to the mountain. Cast it into the sea.*

What kind of mountain are you facing? Does it step out every morning when you get up and shout at you, "You're failing! You're going to die! You're not going to make it...I'm too big...You owe too much...I'm getting bigger every day. I'm a mountain and I'm growing"?

Well, shout back in Jesus' Name! And don't hush. Don't let that mountain get in another word. Every time your mind tries to replay what that mountain said, you take over with God's Words in your words.

Follow David's example. Go to the River (God's Word). Get your smooth stones (God's promises). Put them in your bag (your heart). Put the stone in your sling (your mouth), then run toward the mountain and let the stones fly with all your might.

Knock that mountainous giant in the head. Then climb on its chest and cut its head off with your testimony. Tell everyone that the giant is dead in your life. Don't ever let him get up!

One final note. David took Goliath's armor off. He stripped him. Jesus has stripped the devil of all his armor. You're the one with the battle suit and it's God's armor. Get dressed and move out!

Well, I hope this has thrilled you as much as it has me. In reality *we* are the giants. We are the Body of Christ and it just doesn't get any better than that. Think about that. The Champion of our salvation is also the Lord of our harvest. Open up your heart and let the flood of His grace wash the mountains right into the sea.

Well, it's time to close. Gloria and I love you and pray for you each and every day (and always will).

Love,
Kenneth

February 1992

Don't Join the Recession!
Join the Revival!

Dear Partner,

The world is broadcasting so many bad reports these days that I want to begin this letter today with some great news straight from God's Word.

Acts 2:17-21:

[17]And it shall come to pass in the last days, saith God, I will pour out of my Spirit upon all flesh: and your sons and your daughters shall prophesy, and your young men shall see visions, and your old men shall dream dreams:

[18]And on my servants and on my handmaidens I will pour out in those days of my Spirit; and they shall prophesy:

[19]And I will show wonders in heaven above, and signs in the earth beneath; blood, and fire, and vapour of smoke:

[20]The sun shall be turned into darkness, and the moon into blood, before that great and notable day of the Lord come:

[21]And it shall come to pass, that whosoever shall call on the name of the Lord shall be saved.

God is pouring out His Spirit in greater measure than He has at any time since those words were spoken by the Apostle Peter on the Day of Pentecost. These are those last days Peter prophesied about. Actually, they are the very last of the last days and great things are happening! Of course that's not what you're hearing from the news media and others who are not looking for God's outpouring. But it's true nonetheless. God said He would pour out His Spirit and He is—all over the world!

I know I keep going on about it every time you hear from me, but I can't help it. I'm going to report it! It's happening, glory be to Jesus!

In recent weeks and months, the news media has been reporting heavily about the economic recession that has settled in on our nation. In light of what they're saying, it would seem impossible to escape its effects. But recently I began hearing a phrase in my spirit over and over again, *Don't join the recession.* I began hearing that off and on all day every day. So I began repeating aloud, "I refuse to join the recession."

Then the Lord began talking to me about recessions, setbacks, slowdowns—and all the other different names and phrases people use to describe financial hard places. He reminded me of Philippians 4:19. As I meditated on that scripture, it dawned on me—*My God meets my needs according to His riches in Glory—not according to the condition of the world's economy!*

Why should I join a recession that I don't belong in? I have been redeemed from the curse by the blood of Jesus. I refuse to allow my thinking to be influenced by the constant talk of recession and bad times that is pouring forth from television, newspapers, magazines and mouths of people who have linked themselves to the world's economy.

I'm hearing something other than what the world is saying. I'm hearing, *God is pouring out of His Spirit upon all flesh.* So, as for me and my house, we're joining in with the Word and going with the flow of His outpouring.

You can do the same thing. But as you separate yourself from the world with the Word, just remember to stay in love and forgiveness. Don't get mad at the news media for reporting bad news all the time. That's all they know. You don't have to listen to it, and you certainly don't have to believe what they say.

They don't have the last word on anything, Jesus does. He is the Alpha and the Omega, the First and the Last. So listen to Him and believe His Word. Remember what 3 John 2-4 says?

> **[2]Beloved, I wish above all things that thou mayest prosper and be in health, even as thy soul prospereth.**
> **[3]For I rejoiced greatly, when the brethren came and testified of the truth that is in thee, even as thou walkest in the truth.**
> **[4]I have no greater joy than to hear that my children walk in truth.**

Your prosperity and mine come from the Word and the faith that it produces in our hearts. It is God Who gives the increase (1 Corinthians 3:7).

Since we prosper and walk in health by walking in the Word and keeping ourselves filled with its truths, let's stop right now and look at some more of that truth. Let's look at some good news from heaven—our source—found in Psalm 112:

> [1]Praise ye the Lord. Blessed is the man that feareth the Lord, that delighteth greatly in his commandments.
>
> [2]His seed shall be mighty upon earth: the generation of the upright shall be blessed.
>
> [3]Wealth and riches shall be in his house: and his righteousness endureth for ever.
>
> [4]Unto the upright there ariseth light in the darkness: he is gracious, and full of compassion, and righteous.
>
> [5]A good man showeth favour, and lendeth: he will guide his affairs with discretion.
>
> [6]Surely he shall not be moved for ever: the righteous shall be in everlasting remembrance.
>
> [7]He shall not be afraid of evil tidings: his heart is fixed, trusting in the Lord.
>
> [8]His heart is established, he shall not be afraid, until he see his desire upon his enemies.
>
> [9]He hath dispersed, he hath given to the poor; his righteousness endureth for ever; his horn shall be exalted with honour.
>
> [10]The wicked shall see it, and be grieved; he shall gnash with his teeth, and melt away: the desire of the wicked shall perish.

Notice that the first verse qualifies this entire scripture. All of these great promises are for anyone who reverences and worships God and puts His Word first place in their life. That's what it means to *delight greatly in His commandments.*

Another important thing to notice about the person in Psalm 112 is—he cannot be moved off the Word. He knows God remembers (has a covenant with) him. He pays no attention to bad news because his heart is fixed! His mind is made up! He has settled it forever deep down in his inner man that he has no fear of what the devil does or says in the world around him.

What's more, this person has become a giver instead of a taker. He has solid ground upon which to stand and believe. He knows God honors him because he honors God.

In the days to come, I want you to remember this: *You build your faith in whatever you talk about all the time.* If you talk about recession and bad times, you'll build your faith in its ability to overtake and destroy you. You'll build fear because that's what fear actually is—perverted faith.

Remember what happened to David when he faced Goliath? He continued talking about his victories over the lion and the bear until somebody listened. He kept saying, "I can defeat this giant" until finally King Saul listened to him and believed what he said. David refused to join in with what Goliath had said. Instead, he kept talking his victory until the giant and the whole Philistine army were either dead or had run away.

So fill your heart and your mouth with God's Word and words of your victory in Jesus. Don't join in the recession talk. Don't join in with the defeated. Stay with Jesus and stay in His Word. You can do it. After all, greater is He that is in you than he that is in the world.

Get a note card and write Psalm 112 on it. Put your name in every verse. Then post it on the refrigerator door or someplace where you'll see it every day. Read it out loud and then shout:

> *Yes, that's me! I'm not afraid of evil tidings—whatever they are. My heart is fixed. I'm trusting in God forever. I'm not joining the recession. I'm joining the revival. Jesus, You are Lord. I'm staying with You!*

The days ahead are going to be the biggest, fullest days of our lives. Together, as Partners in God's work we have much to do, much to give and much to receive. So when you sow your financial seeds, take a moment to see in your spirit your offerings flowing into a huge river of the givings of God's people. See them flowing through the very throne room of God, and out from there into this great end-time harvest of souls. I wish I could put on paper what I'm seeing right now. I can't, so just lay your hands on this letter and ask God to let you see it too.

A flood of God's greatest blessing is crashing like a mighty ocean wave all over this nation and all over the world. It's just as much yours as it is mine or anyone else's. Receive it now. It's yours in Jesus' Name.

Thank you for praying for Gloria and me and this ministry. We love you and pray for you every day.

Love,
Ken

November 1990

Dwell in the Secret Place

Dear Partner,

He that dwells in the secret place of the most High shall abide under the shadow of the Almighty.

That grand statement is, of course, the first verse of the 91st Psalm which has been a favorite of Gloria's and mine for many years. I've studied it, quoted it, confessed it, prayed it, shouted it and even sometimes cried it out before the throne of grace.

However, it has exploded inside me with one revelation after another since I began praying it every day for you and all our other Partners. Let me take you through this powerful psalm and share some of the things that I have received from it.

Look at verse 1: *"He that dwelleth in the secret place of the most High shall abide under the shadow of the Almighty."* Notice that our dwelling place of security is in God's shadow. That means that He is bigger than we are. He is big enough to cast a shadow over the entire Body of Christ. Anywhere you are, all you have to do is look over your shoulder, look up—and He's there! He's always there!

Before we look at the rest of the verses, remember what Jesus said in Matthew 10:32. *"Whosoever therefore shall confess me before men, him will I also confess before my Father which is in heaven."* Then in Luke 12:8 He said, *"Whosoever shall confess me before men, him shall the Son of man also* confess *before the angels of God."* What you say here on Earth causes supernatural things to happen in heaven.

No wonder Psalm 91:2 begins with the words *I will say!*

²I will say of the Lord, He is my refuge and my fortress: my God; in him will I trust.

³Surely he shall deliver thee from the snare of the fowler, and from the noisome pestilence.

⁴He shall cover thee with his feathers, and under his wings shalt thou trust: his truth shall be thy shield and buckler.

⁵Thou shalt not be afraid for the terror by night; nor for the arrow that flieth by day;

⁶Nor for the pestilence that walketh in darkness; nor for the destruction that wasteth at noonday.

⁷A thousand shall fall at thy side, and ten thousand at thy right hand; but it shall not come nigh thee.

⁸Only with thine eyes shalt thou behold and see the reward of the wicked.

⁹Because thou hast made the Lord, which is my refuge, even the most High, thy habitation;

[10]There shall no evil befall thee, neither shall any plague come nigh thy dwelling.

[11]For he shall give his angels charge over thee, to keep thee in *all* thy ways.

[12]They shall bear thee up in their hands, lest thou dash thy foot against a stone.

[13]Thou shalt tread upon the lion and adder: the young lion and the dragon shalt thou trample under feet.

[14]Because he hath set his love upon me, therefore will I deliver him: I will set him on high, because he hath known my name.

[15]He shall call upon me, and I will answer him: I will be with him in trouble; I will deliver him, and honour him.

[16]With long life will I satisfy him, and show him my salvation.

Notice, verse 2 is our confession. If we won't or don't say these things, then the rest of the psalm will never work for us because Jesus is the High Priest of our confession. His confession comes in response to ours (Hebrews 3:1).

All we have to do is say, "He is my refuge. He is my fortress. He is my God. In Him I do trust."

Then immediately Jesus begins to speak in verse 3 and say, *"Surely He [God the Father] shall deliver thee...."* Then He continues *His confession* before the Father about us in response to *our confession* before men about Him.

In verses 11 and 12, Jesus makes a confession before the

Father about the ministry of angels and what they are charged to do concerning those of us who "say of the Lord."

If all that wasn't exciting enough, look at verse 14. Now the Father is speaking in response to Jesus' confession before Him:

Because he hath set his love upon me, therefore will I deliver Him: I will set him on high, because he hath known my name. He shall call upon me, and I will answer him: I will be with him in trouble; I will deliver him, and honour him. With long life will I satisfy him, and show him my salvation.

Now go back and read the whole psalm and put your name in it. Read it aloud over and over again. If you have loved ones who are facing danger, either copy this letter and send it to them, or copy it in your own handwriting and send it.

I am praying this psalm for you every day along with the other scripture prayers that we have been praying for you for a long time.

This is a powerful, life-changing word from God that I intend to continue for the rest of my life. It's a daily thing with me from now on. I strongly urge you to make the same commitment to it in your life. The more you "say of the Lord," the more each verse comes alive with the anointing of the Holy Spirit.

My, we are experiencing such revival here at KCM. Everything is going wide open, and I know it's because of the flood of prayer and faith that's flowing through heaven from the prayers of our Partners.

I don't have words to tell you how strong Gloria and I have become in recent weeks right in the middle of some of the busiest times we have ever had. Our staff has grown in and been strengthened in the Spirit more than I have ever seen, and I want to thank you and all of our other Partners for being so faithful to pray and hold us up.

These are critical but powerful days. We are in them together, and we will win together. *Together*, we can do anything through Christ Jesus Who is our strength.

I say of the Lord:

> He is our refuge.
> He is our fortress.
> He is our God.
> In Him will we trust.

Gloria and I love you more every time we pray for you.

JESUS IS LORD!
Kenneth

March 1992

You Haven't Failed Until You Quit

Dear Partner,

There are wonderful things going on in many parts of the world right now. Things only God could bring to pass. There's an avalanche of souls flooding into the kingdom of God in nations all over the world. So many in some places that it's almost impossible to handle such overwhelming numbers.

"But why aren't we seeing that in the USA?" several people have asked me. My answer has been twofold.

First, maybe you're looking in the wrong places. There are more people coming to Jesus in the United States now than ever. However, there are more good churches, more people praying and so many more people to handle the new souls that are coming in, that it isn't overwhelming and it doesn't look like a flood—*yet!*

Second, that flood is coming. It's building now toward an explosion of an outpouring of Holy Ghost power. It will eventually be just as overwhelming here as it is in Russia now. And when we get an overwhelming sweep of God's hand in this country, it is really going to be something. It's coming and, thank God, you and I will be right in the middle of it! What a privilege!

Isn't God's grace wonderful?

I don't care how badly you've messed up or how worthless you may feel you are to God—He'll never get through with you. He'll never throw you away. He'll never leave you nor forsake you. Sometimes I wonder how He puts up with me. But, thank God, He does, and He just keeps working with me to improve my life and keep me in victory in Jesus.

Don't ever get the idea that you're the only one who ever does stupid things or that everyone else is walking in flawless faith while you're stumbling around all over the place. That's just not true. All of us have done a lot of stumbling and falling around. We're all under a lot of pressure from a lot of different directions.

You would feel much differently about yourself if you could see into the spirit world and see the vast array of evil spirits and weapons that have been thrown at you by the devil. You've probably done a whole lot better job standing against them than you thought you did.

But what difference does it make now even if you've been a total flop? None!

God loves you. Jesus is ever making intercession for you. His precious blood still stands in your behalf. His Word still works and it's still available.

No matter how many times you have missed the mark, stand up and reach for God's best. It's still there for you. Bombard bad feelings of guilt and loss with a big mouthful of God's Word. Lean hard on God's grace and mercy. It will hold you up. His love for you is just as great now as it ever was.

You and I are more than conquerors in Jesus—whether

YOU HAVEN'T FAILED UNTIL YOU QUIT | 207

we look like it at the moment or not. That's not what we are trying to become, that's what we are!

I want to give you some steps to victory in Jesus that I learned many years ago. They have always worked when I have put them to work and they will always work for you. They work because they are God's Word.

Step 1: Go to the promise in God's Word that covers your situation. Start by reading 2 Peter 1:1-10.

> [1] Simon Peter, a servant and an apostle of Jesus Christ, to them that have obtained like precious faith with us through the righteousness of God and our Savior Jesus Christ:
>
> [2] Grace and peace be multiplied unto you through the knowledge of God, and of Jesus our Lord,
>
> [3] According as his divine power hath given unto us all things that pertain unto life and godliness, through the knowledge of him that hath called us to glory and virtue:
>
> [4] Whereby are given unto us exceeding great and precious promises: that by these ye might be partakers of the divine nature, having escaped the corruption that is in the world through lust.
>
> [5] And beside this, giving all diligence add to your faith virtue; and to virtue knowledge;
>
> [6] And to knowledge temperance; and to temperance patience; and to patience godliness;

[7] And to godliness brotherly kindness; and to brotherly kindness charity.

[8] For if these things be in you, and abound, they make you that ye shall neither be barren nor unfruitful in the knowledge of our Lord Jesus Christ.

[9] But he that lacketh these things is blind, and cannot see afar off, and hath forgotten that he was purged from his old sins.

[10] Wherefore the rather, brethren, give diligence to make your calling and election sure: for if ye do these things, ye shall never fall.

Look at that fourth verse again. It says we've been given great and precious promises. So, search the New Testament again like you have never read it before. As you do, be sensitive to the Holy Spirit. He will quicken verses of Scripture to your heart that are just for you. Make notes of them and go back to them again and again so that the Lord Jesus can minister to you through them.

Then start at verse 5 of 2 Peter 1 and go through verse 7, doing what each verse says to do. After you've done that, stand firmly on verses 8, 9 and 10. In fact, look at verse 10 right now and shout! *You shall never fall!* With a promise like that, it's all done but the doing.

Step 2: Keep the promises that you've found during your search of the New Testament before your eyes, in your ears and in your mouth.

[20]My son, attend to my words; incline thine ear unto my sayings.

[21]Let them not depart from thine eyes; keep them in the midst of thine heart.

[22]For they are life unto those that find them, and health to all their flesh.

[23]Keep thy heart with all diligence; for out of it are the issues of life.

[24]Put away from thee a froward [disobedient] mouth, and perverse lips put far from thee.

[25]Let thine eyes look right on, and let thine eyelids look straight before thee (Proverbs 4:20-25).

Step 3: Go to God on the basis of His provision, not on the basis of your need.

God is no longer moved to action by our great needs. He has already moved to meet those needs. He did that when Jesus went to the cross. Our faith in His work at the cross, in Jesus and in His written Word, is what moves Him now. We must pray God's promises before Him just like Jesus did. "It is written" is far more powerful than "Oh God, I'm so sick" or "I'm so broke."

Step 4: Speak to the mountain. Speak those promises directly to the mountain of sickness and disease, or whatever is threatening your life and peace in Jesus. Command it to be removed and cast into the sea like Jesus said in Mark 11:23.

Step 5: Praise continually. Start right now whether you feel like it or not. You may have to literally bulldoze your way through your feelings. That's all right, do it. Bow your spiritual neck and plow your way through all that resistance. Charge! Satan will always flee. He must. The Word says so.

A pastor friend of mine, big Tom Slayton, said to me, "No matter what you've done, you haven't failed until you give up and quit." That's so true. The Word never fails. The blood never fails. And the Name of Jesus never fails—unless we quit and throw them down saying, "It's all over for me." That's what Satan is trying to get us to do, because that's the only way he can win.

So don't do that! Instead, act on these steps to victory and you'll be shocked at how rapidly things start happening around you.

Well, I must close. Please hold Gloria and me up in prayer, especially in the area of ministry decisions. We are acting on these steps for God's guidance. We love you and pray for you every day.

Love,
Ken

April 1992

A Right Decision Made Is a Victory Won

Dear Partner,

Recently, the Lord has made me very aware of the importance of making right decisions. He's revealed to me that too many decisions in our lives are being made as reactions instead of as the result of prayer.

It's the quality of our decisions that determines the level of our commitment to the Lord and to the things He has called us to do. In Luke 12:16-20, Jesus tells of a man who made a poor decision. Let's read what He said.

[16] **And he spake a parable unto them, saying, The ground of a certain rich man brought forth plentifully:**

[17] **And he thought within himself, saying, What shall I do, because I have no room where to bestow my fruits?**

[18] **And he said, This will I do: I will pull down my barns, and build greater; and there will I bestow all my fruits and my goods.**

[19] **And I will say to my soul, Soul, thou hast much goods laid up for many years; take thine ease, eat, drink, and be merry.**

²⁰But God said unto him, Thou fool, this night thy soul shall be required of thee: then whose shall those things be which thou hast provided?

Notice in this scripture that the abundance brought forth from this man's ground was not what got him into trouble. (After all, according to Deuteronomy 8:18, *"It is* He [God] *that giveth thee power to get wealth.")* No, what got this man in trouble was the fact that *"He thought within himself."* He made a decision. He made it with only himself in mind.

It's obvious he didn't consult God about it because leaving God out is really what got him into trouble. He didn't trust God at all. He made his decisions in his own wisdom. Thank God, we don't have to do that. First Corinthians 1:30 says, *"God has made Jesus unto us wisdom."* His wisdom is available both in His Word and inside our spirits.

Look at Ephesians 4:28:

Let him that stole steal no more: but rather let him labour, working with his hands the thing which is good, that he may have to give to him that needeth.

If the rich man in Jesus' parable had been Word of God-minded, he would have been giving and trusting God. But instead, his only goal in life was to "keep, keep, store up and see how much I can get for me." The time came to change all that and he missed his opportunity.

The time for us to change *our* decision making is now!

We learn how to make good decisions in life by making them on a daily basis—not by waiting until some large, life-threatening situation is staring us in the face. Being Word of God-minded and being sensitive to the Holy Spirit's leading in the daily decisions of life prepares and trains us for the time when the big decisions come.

In fact, becoming Word-minded makes most decision making easy because the Word will make the right decision for us. We don't have to wonder about something when we already know what the Word says about it.

However, even that takes a decision of quality. We must decide we're going to do whatever the Word says every time. We must decide in advance that regardless of what it looks like might happen, God is always right! He *is*, you know! And His Word always works to our advantage—never to our disadvantage—regardless of how hard the devil tries to scramble the circumstances to make it look like the Word won't work this time.

A quality decision, one from which there is no retreat and about which there is no argument, is the most powerful thing God has given us.

Once you decided to make Jesus your Lord, all the devils in hell could not stop the new birth from taking place in your life. The same is true concerning receiving all the promises of God. God has done everything it takes for our lives to be successful. He sent Jesus to the cross and raised Him from the dead. All we have to do is make the decision to receive His promises and provisions and to walk in them by faith.

There is so much going on right now in the spirit realm that many decisions must be made to stick close to Jesus and to one another in the Lord.

These are dangerous times and these are glorious times. Making the right decisions will have a great effect not only on our own lives, but also on the Body of Christ.

Lay your hands on this letter right now and believe God for His wisdom to make the right decisions in your life. Gloria and I are in agreement with you for God's very best.

We love you and pray for you every day.

Love,
Ken

May 1992

Your Future Is Inside You Right Now

Dear Partner,

In the past few days, economists have announced that the recession is over. Thank God! It just couldn't stand up to all that prayer and faith. However, this is no time to let up on our believing where our finances are concerned. This is no time to relax our stand.

"Well, Brother Copeland, when can we relax our stand? When can we let up on our fighting the good fight of faith?"

Never! Not while we're on this Earth! We must keep the pressure on the devil all the time. That way, we not only overcome when times are tough, we excel when Satan draws back and flees!

In this letter I want to share something with you beginning with John 17:14-17:

> **[14]I have given them thy word; and the world hath hated them, because they are not of the world, even as I am not of the world.**
> **[15]I pray not that thou shouldest take them out of the world, but that thou shouldest keep them from the evil.**

¹⁶**They are not of the world, even as I am not of the world.**

¹⁷**Sanctify them through thy truth: thy word is truth.**

Notice the word *sanctify* in verse 17. It means to *separate unto God.* "Separate them through thy truth: thy word is truth."

In John 8:23, Jesus told unbelievers, *"Ye are from beneath, I am from above: ye are of this world: I am not of this world."* Then, the moment many of them believed on Him He said, *"If ye continue in my word, then are ye my disciples indeed: And ye shall know the truth, and the truth shall make you free"* (verses 31-32).

First Peter 1:23 says we have been born again by the incorruptible seed of the Word of God. Colossians 1:13 says we have been delivered from the authority of darkness and translated (or separated) into the kingdom of God's dear Son.

Put those truths all together and you'll see that as believers, you and I don't belong to this world and all its problems. We don't belong to sin and death, and it doesn't belong to us. We don't belong to sickness and disease. We don't belong to the money lenders. Debt ties us back to the world's system with its crashes, recessions, wipeouts, homelessness, unemployment and all of the pain that financial problems can bring. That system is cursed by the same law of sin and death that curses everything else in this natural world.

But we've been delivered from that curse! For the law of the spirit of life has made us free from the law of sin and death (Romans 8:2).

The Word of God made us free when we were born again and the Word will keep us free as long as we walk in it, stand on it, confess it with our mouths and feed our spirits with it continuously.

Jesus, referring to the Word of God in Luke 11:49, called the Word the *Wisdom of God.* That Wisdom is what enables us to live without being bound to this world's system of death.

God's Wisdom is your future. Without His Wisdom you'll never know what to do or how to do it except by the world's ways. And the world has already failed. Its system is bankrupt in every area.

Gloria said something a few days ago that just thrilled my spirit. She said, "Your future is inside you now." Think about that. You can constantly feed your spirit and mind on God's Wisdom or on the world's wisdom. You can choose either one. But remember, whatever you put inside you determines your future.

Jesus said it this way in Mark 4:24: *"Take heed what ye hear: with what measure ye mete, it shall be measured to you: and unto you that hear shall more be given."* He also said, *"Out of the abundance of the heart the mouth speaketh. A good man out of the good treasure of the heart bringeth forth good things: and an evil man out of the evil treasure bringeth forth evil things"* (Matthew 12:34-35).

Your future is in your heart and in your mouth!

Take a look at what you're spending most of your time

listening to and watching. Is it filled with love and faith and a sound mind? Look at it! It's your future.

Do you like the direction your life is headed? Do you want to change it? Then change the seed you're planting in the soil of your heart because that's where it all begins. Jesus gave his life so that we could be separated from this world of sin and death. So let's give ourselves to staying free by His Word and helping others to be made free as well.

As you sow your financial seeds into the work of God in the days ahead, give as a seed of faith toward your future in Jesus in this earth. A seed of determination to make your time count in His Word. Stay with it, and the Word will stay with you.

Gloria and I love you and pray for you every day.

Love,
Ken

June 1992

Be Like Jesus—Be Free!

Dear Partner,

The great God of the universe, the almighty living God has given Himself to you and me to be our Father. Isn't that an awesome thought? If you're like me you need to hear that and meditate on it all the time—not just after something has gone wrong, but all the time.

The more you think about Jesus being your very own Brother and God being your Father, the more real Their presence becomes inside you. The more you meditate on God's Word, the more you see into it and understand how to do what is written there. God told Joshua that kind of meditation on the Word would make him very strong and courageous. It will do the same for you.

You can think about the Word in everything you do all day long. Regardless of what you're doing, God's Word has something to say about it or applies to it in some way.

When you're doing something and you don't know how the Word applies to it, stop for a moment and ask God for His wisdom and insight into the situation. Ask Him what the Word has to say about it. That's not only a great way to learn more about the Word of God, it's also the way to learn more about whatever you're doing.

Jesus said the Holy Spirit would lead and guide us into all

truth. That's really the secret to a rich, full, God-filled life on this Earth.

Now, get your Bible and let's look at something Jesus said in John 8:26-29:

> [26] I have many things to say and to judge of you: but he that sent me is true; and I speak to the world those things which I have heard of him.
>
> [27] They understood not that he spake to them of the Father.
>
> [28] Then said Jesus unto them, When ye have lifted up the Son of man, then shall ye know that I am he, and that I do nothing of myself; but as my Father hath taught me, I speak these things.
>
> [29] And he that sent me is with me: the Father hath not left me alone; for I do always those things that please him.

Notice what Jesus said in verse 26: *"He that sent me is true; and I speak to the world those things which I have heard of him."* Now look at verse 28: *"I do nothing of myself; but as my Father hath taught me, I speak these things."* Then in verse 29 He said, *"I do always those things that please him."*

Jesus said only what the Father, or the True One, said, therefore, what He said was true. Jesus did only what the Father said to do, therefore, what Jesus did was always right.

If Jesus had stopped there after verse 29, we would have

to say, "My, that's wonderful, but what does it have to do with me?"

But He didn't stop there. He went on to say, *"If ye continue in my word [which is the Word of the Father], then are ye my disciples indeed; And ye shall know the truth, and the truth shall make you free"* (verses 31-32).

What Jesus was telling us is this: He perfectly imitated the Father the same way we imitate Him—with God's written Word. For example, when Jesus was face to face with Satan, all He would say was, *"It is written...."* And when He said in John 8:28, *"As my Father hath taught me, I speak these things,"* He was referring to the written Word. Jesus learned from the written Word by the Holy Spirit's teaching and guiding just like you and I do.

Jesus lived in freedom from the death cycle of the world. He lived in freedom from sin, sickness, poverty and every other part of the curse—and He did it not by some special power He had because He was the Son of God, but by perfectly walking in the Word of God.

So when He said, *"Continue ye in My Word,"* He was telling us, *"Say what I say, do what I do, and you'll be like Me—you'll be free. You won't be tied to the world and to its cycle of sin and death."*

You might say, "Oh, that sounds hard! I don't think I could ever do that." Why not? According to John 8:30, Jesus said those words to people who had only been believers a few seconds. If He expected them to be able to imitate Him, surely you can too!

How? The same way you would imitate an instructor who was teaching you how to speak another language, drive a car, play a sport, or anything else. You say what your instructor—Jesus—says. You do what He does, and you do it and say it as closely as you can to the way He does it and says it. You copy Him every way you can. You keep doing that and you will eventually become like Him.

Jesus taught in Matthew 7:24-27 that if we act like a wise man (God), we get a wise man's results and reward. If we act like a fool (the devil), we reap a fool's harvest and destruction.

So act like God does! Say what He has already said in His Word about every situation in your life. Say it to God and say it to the situation. Say it to yourself and say it to the devil until the situation changes.

God's Word will never change. God will never change. If you don't let go of the Word, you become unchangeable. That only leaves the devil and the situation. The devil will flee and the situation has no choice. It must change.

You are free! The truth has made you free, just like Jesus. Remember, He is appointed of God as the High Priest of our confession of faith (Hebrews 3:1). It's His responsibility to see to it that the Word of God, which we speak, comes to pass. So get busy. Give Him something to bring to pass. Speak the Word boldly.

Speak it to God!

Speak it to yourself!

Speak it to the situation (sickness, poverty, death, etc.)!

Speak it to the devil—let him know that you are free!

Well, I certainly hope this letter is a blessing to you. Read it over several times in the days ahead and let the truth of it take root in you. Then put these principles into operation.

Keep speaking the Word and rejoicing every day. Faith will rise to a new level and so will you!

Gloria and I love you and pray for you every day.

Love,
Ken

July 1992

We Are Partners
in the Victory of Jesus!

Dear Partner,

As I write this letter, it is springtime and Gloria and I are at our prayer cabin in Arkansas. This place is so beautiful this time of year. All the new life is so vibrant. The flowers are in full bloom. The trees are plush and green and all the animals have their newborns out running around.

Everything is so alive!

It is obvious that God is the source of life. Life is such a beautiful thing, and death and suffering are such repulsive acts of the devil. No wonder God is against death and sin. Jesus came that we might have life and have it more abundantly.

Every time Gloria and I come up here, we sense you and all the rest of our Partners strongly and heavily on our hearts. It's not the kind of heaviness that comes when something bad is happening, but the fullness of the presence of the Holy Spirit hanging heavily and close. I know we experience that because we've had so many special times of prayer for you here at our prayer cabin.

Another thing I become so aware of when I'm here is the faithfulness of our Partners—your faithfulness to pray and stand with us in this ministry through thick and thin. Gloria

and I believe without a doubt we have the most faithful
Partners of any ministry in the world. I'm not just saying
that to flatter or to be nice. I really believe it. That's why we
can stand so firmly before the Lord on scriptures such as
Ephesians 6:8:

> **Knowing that whatsoever good thing any
> man doeth, the same shall he receive of the
> Lord, whether he be bond or free.**

I was reading this morning from 1 Samuel 30:1-25. It tells
of the time when David and his army were away at battle
and the Amalekites invaded their home base of Ziklag, taking captive all their wives and children and burning their
homes to the ground. In response to that invasion, David
took 600 men and set out on a forced march to catch up with
the Amalekite army. They marched until they came to a
ravine called Besor.

Two hundred of the men were so worn out from the
forced march they couldn't cross the ravine. So David left
them there to watch over the supplies. Then David and 400
men crossed the Besor and caught up with the Amalekites.
After about 24 straight hours of combat, David totally
defeated his enemy and recovered all of his men's families
and goods unharmed.

Now let's look at verses 20-25:

> [20]**And David took all the flocks and the herds,
> which they drave before those other cattle, and
> said, This is David's spoil.**

[21]And David came to the two hundred men, which were so faint that they could not follow David, whom they had made also to abide at the brook Besor: and they went forth to meet David, and to meet the people that were with him: and when David came near to the people, he saluted them.

[22]Then answered all the wicked men and men of Belial, of those that went with David, and said, Because they went not with us, we will not give them aught of the spoil that we have recovered, save to every man his wife and his children, that they may lead them away, and depart.

[23]Then said David, Ye shall not do so, my brethren, with that which the Lord hath given us, who hath preserved us, and delivered the company that came against us into our hand.

[24]For who will hearken unto you in this matter? but as his part is that goeth down to the battle, so shall his part be that tarrieth by the stuff: they shall part alike.

[25]And it was so from that day forward, that he made it a statute and an ordinance for Israel unto this day.

Notice that verse 24 says the spoils of victory must be shared alike between those who are on the front line and those in the rear. This is the verse of Scripture the Lord laid on my heart years ago when I first began inviting Partners into this ministry.

He instructed Gloria and me that our Partners would share in every blessing and reward we receive for preaching His Word on the front lines around the world. He said that those who help make it possible for us to go would share equally in the victories.

That means you receive credit in God's eyes for every person who is born again through this ministry, every person set free by the Word of God, every person delivered, every baby saved from starving to death, every person who will not freeze because we provided a coat for his back, food on his table, a blanket on his bed, and most important of all, teaching from the Word of God that will enable him to live by faith so those provisions can keep coming.

There are great blessings and rewards—both heavenly and earthly—for being obedient to God's voice and allowing Him to bring these things to pass. These rewards are just as much yours as they are ours. In Philippians 1:7 the Apostle Paul said to his partners:

Even as it is meet for me to think this of you all, because I have you in my heart; inasmuch as both in my bonds, and in the defence and confirmation of the gospel, ye all are partakers of my grace.

Paul said his partners partook of the same grace that worked to confirm the gospel when he preached it. Mark 16:20 says the confirmation of the Word preached is "signs

following." In other words, Paul's partners were even partakers of the miracles that followed his ministry! This is the
foundational truth of Philippians 4:19. Because his partners
had invested in his ministry, Paul knew they had blessings
"on account" with God. So he could say with boldness, *"My
God shall supply all your need according to his riches in
glory by Christ Jesus."*

The same is true for you. You are our Partners! We are
in this together! The grace that follows us, follows you!
And you have a harvest of blessing on account to meet
your needs!

This ministry is growing by leaps and bounds. It is reaching into places with the message of Jesus and the power of
His Word that I never thought it would. I knew the Word
would go to those places, but I didn't know it would be this
ministry that would take it there.

I don't have time or space to tell you all of the ways this
ministry is spreading the gospel. But that's not really the
main point here. What I primarily want to do today is
encourage you to reach out in faith to receive your blessings
and rewards. They are yours. Believe you receive them now.

I know you've probably heard me say all these things
before, but I want (actually the Lord wants) them to be
fresh in your heart and mind. Every time you sow a financial seed into this ministry, remember the spiritual laws
I've shared with you today. Go back over this letter and read
it again and again until they're etched on your heart.

You and I are part of something bigger than we can ever
imagine. We are a vital working part of the Body of Jesus—the
anointed Son of the Living God. We are part of His victory!

Gloria and I love you and pray for you every day...and always will.

Love,
Ken

Partners in Prayer

Through the years of writing letters to his Partners, God has given Brother Copeland specific scriptures to stand on as he prays for them every day. These scriptures are how he prays for their well-being—spirit, soul and body.

Psalm 23

The Lord is my shepherd; I shall not want. He maketh me to lie down in green pastures: he leadeth me beside the still waters. He restoreth my soul: he leadeth me in the paths of righteousness for his name's sake. Yea, though I walk through the valley of the shadow of death, I will fear no evil: for thou art with me; thy rod and thy staff they comfort me. Thou preparest a table before me in the presence of mine enemies: thou anointest my head with oil; my cup runneth over. Surely goodness and mercy shall follow me all the days of my life: and I will dwell in the house of the Lord for ever.

Psalm 91

He that dwelleth in the secret place of the most High shall abide under the shadow of the Almighty. I will say of the Lord, He is my refuge and my fortress: my God; in him will I trust. Surely he shall deliver thee from the snare of the fowler, and from the noisome pestilence. He shall cover thee with his feathers, and under his wings shalt thou trust: his truth shall be thy shield and buckler. Thou shalt not be afraid for the terror by night; nor for the arrow that flieth by day; Nor for the pestilence that walketh in darkness; nor for the destruction that wasteth at noonday. A thousand shall fall at thy side, and ten thousand at thy right hand; but it shall not come nigh thee. Only with thine eyes shalt thou behold and see the reward of the wicked.

Because thou hast made the Lord, which is my refuge, even the most High, thy habitation; There shall no evil befall thee, neither shall any plague come nigh thy dwelling. For he shall give his angels charge over thee, to keep thee in all thy ways. They shall bear thee up in their hands, lest thou dash thy foot against a stone. Thou shalt tread upon the lion and adder: the young lion and the dragon shalt thou trample under feet. Because he hath set his love upon me, therefore will I deliver him: I will set him on high, because he hath known my name. He shall call upon me, and I will answer him: I will be with him in trouble; I will deliver him, and honour him.

With long life will I satisfy him, and show him my salvation.

Psalm 103

Bless the Lord, O my soul: and all that is within me, bless his holy name. Bless the Lord, O my soul, and forget not all his benefits: Who forgiveth all thine iniquities; who healeth all thy diseases; Who redeemeth thy life from destruction; who crowneth thee with lovingkindness and tender mercies; Who satisfieth thy mouth with good things; so that thy youth is renewed like the eagle's.

The Lord executeth righteousness and judgment for all that are oppressed. He made known his ways unto Moses, his acts unto the children of Israel. The Lord is merciful and gracious, slow to anger, and plenteous in mercy. He will not always chide: neither will he keep his anger for ever. He hath not dealt with us after our sins; nor rewarded us according to our iniquities. For as the heaven is high above the earth, so great is his mercy toward them that fear him. As far as the east is from the west, so far hath he removed our transgressions from us. Like as a father pitieth his children, so the Lord pitieth them that fear him. For he knoweth our frame; he remembereth that we are dust. As for man, his days are as grass: as a flower of the field, so he flourisheth. For the wind passeth over it, and it is gone; and the place thereof shall know it no more. But the mercy of the Lord is from everlasting to everlasting upon them that fear him, and his righteousness unto children's children; To such as keep his covenant, and to those that remember his commandments to do them.

The Lord hath prepared his throne in the heavens; and his kingdom ruleth over all. Bless the Lord, ye his angels, that excel in strength, that do his commandments, hearkening unto the voice of his word. Bless ye the Lord, all ye his hosts; ye ministers of his, that do his pleasure. Bless the Lord, all his works in all places of his dominion: bless the Lord, O my soul.

Isaiah 54:8-17

In a little wrath I hid my face from thee for a moment; but with everlasting kindness will I have mercy on thee, saith the Lord thy Redeemer. For this is as the waters of Noah unto me: for as I have sworn that the waters of Noah should no more go over the earth; so have I sworn that I would not be wroth with thee, nor rebuke thee. For the mountains shall depart, and the hills be removed; but my kindness shall not depart from thee, neither shall the covenant of my peace be removed, saith the Lord that hath mercy on thee.

O thou afflicted, tossed with tempest, and not comforted, behold, I will lay thy stones with fair colours, and lay thy foundations with sapphires. And I will make thy windows of agates, and thy gates of carbuncles, and all thy borders of pleasant stones. And all thy children shall be taught of the Lord; and great shall be the peace of thy children. In righteousness shalt thou be established: thou shalt be far from oppression; for thou shalt not fear: and from terror; for it shall not come near thee. Behold, they shall surely gather together, but not by me: whosoever shall gather together against thee shall fall for thy sake. Behold, I have created the smith that bloweth the coals in the fire, and that bringeth forth an instrument for his work; and I have created the waster to destroy. No weapon that is formed against thee shall prosper; and every tongue that shall rise against thee in judgment thou shalt condemn. This is the heritage of the servants of the Lord, and their righteousness is of me, saith the Lord.

Ephesians 1:16-23

[I] cease not to give thanks for you, making mention of you in my prayers; That the God of our Lord Jesus Christ, the Father of glory, may give unto you the spirit of wisdom and revelation in the knowledge of him: The eyes of your understanding being enlightened; that ye may know what is the hope of his calling, and what the riches of the glory of his inheritance in the saints, And what is the exceeding greatness of his power to us-ward who believe, according to the working of his mighty power, Which he wrought in Christ, when he raised him from the dead, and set him at his own right hand in

the heavenly places, Far above all principality, and power, and might, and dominion, and every name that is named, not only in this world, but also in that which is to come: And hath put all things under his feet, and gave him to be the head over all things to the church, Which is his body, the fulness of him that filleth all in all.

Ephesians 3:14-20

For this cause I bow my knees unto the Father of our Lord Jesus Christ, Of whom the whole family in heaven and earth is named, That he would grant you, according to the riches of his glory, to be strengthened with might by his Spirit in the inner man; That Christ may dwell in your hearts by faith; that ye, being rooted and grounded in love, May be able to comprehend with all saints what is the breadth, and length, and depth, and height; And to know the love of Christ, which passeth knowledge, that ye might be filled with all the fulness of God. Now unto him that is able to do exceeding abundantly above all that we ask or think, according to the power that worketh in us.

Colossians 1:9-11

For this cause we also, since the day we heard it, do not cease to pray for you, and to desire that ye might be filled with the knowledge of his will in all wisdom and spiritual understanding; That ye might walk worthy of the Lord unto all pleasing, being fruitful in every good work, and increasing in the knowledge of God; Strengthened with all might, according to his glorious power, unto all patience and longsuffering with joyfulness.

Prayer for Salvation and Baptism in the Holy Spirit

Heavenly Father, I come to You in the Name of Jesus. Your Word says, *"Whosoever shall call on the name of the Lord shall be saved"* (Acts 2:21). I am calling on You. I pray and ask Jesus to come into my heart and be Lord over my life according to Romans 10:9-10. *"If thou shalt confess with thy mouth the Lord Jesus, and shalt believe in thine heart that God hath raised him from the dead, thou shalt be saved."* I do that now. I confess that Jesus is Lord, and I believe in my heart that God raised Him from the dead.

I am now reborn! I am a Christian—a child of Almighty God! I am saved! You also said in Your Word, *"If ye then, being evil, know how to give good gifts unto your children: HOW MUCH MORE shall your heavenly Father give the Holy Spirit to them that ask him?"* (Luke 11:13). I'm also asking You to fill me with the Holy Spirit. Holy Spirit, rise up within me as I praise God. I fully expect to speak with other tongues as You give me the utterance (Acts 2:4).

Begin to praise God for filling you with the Holy Spirit. Speak those words and syllables you receive—not in your own language, but the language given to you by the Holy Spirit. You have to use your own voice. God will not force you to speak. Worship and praise Him in your heavenly language—in other tongues.

Continue with the blessing God has given you and pray in tongues each day.

You are a born-again, Spirit-filled believer. You'll never be the same!

Find a good Word of God preaching church, and become a part of a church family who will love and care for you as you love and care for them.

We need to be hooked up to each other. It increases our strength in God. It's God's plan for us.

About the Author

Kenneth Copeland is co-founder and president of Kenneth Copeland Ministries in Fort Worth, Texas, and best-selling author of books that include *Managing God's Mutual Funds, How to Discipline Your Flesh* and *Honor—Walking in Honesty, Truth and Integrity.*

Now in his 30th year as minister of the gospel of Christ and teacher of God's Word, Kenneth is the recording artist of such award-winning albums as his Grammy nominated *Only the Redeemed, In His Presence, He Is Jehovah* and his most recently released *I Was On His Mind.* He also co-stars as the character Wichita Slim in the children's adventure videos *The Gunslinger, Covenant Rider* and the movie *Treasure of Eagle Mountain* and as Daniel Lyon in the Commander Kellie and the Superkids_{SM} video *Armor of Light.*

With the help of offices and staff in the United States, Canada, England, Australia, South Africa and Ukraine, Kenneth is fulfilling his vision to boldly preach the uncompromised Word of God from the top of this world, to the bottom, and all the way around. His ministry reaches millions of people worldwide through daily and weekly TV broadcasts, magazines, audio and video teaching tapes, conventions and campaigns.

Books by Kenneth Copeland

* A Ceremony of Marriage
  A Matter of Choice
  Covenant of Blood
  Faith and Patience—The Power Twins
* Freedom From Fear
  From Faith to Faith—A Daily Guide to Victory
  Giving and Receiving
  Healing Promises
  Honor—Walking in Honesty, Truth & Integrity
  How to Conquer Strife
  How to Discipline Your Flesh
  How to Receive Communion
  Love Never Fails
  Managing God's Mutual Funds
* Now Are We in Christ Jesus
* Our Covenant With God
* Prayer—Your Foundation for Success
  Prosperity Promises
  Prosperity: The Choice Is Yours
  Rumors of War
* Sensitivity of Heart
  Six Steps to Excellence in Ministry
  Sorrow Not! Winning Over Grief and Sorrow
* The Decision Is Yours
* The Force of Faith
* The Force of Righteousness
  The Image of God in You
  The Laws of Prosperity
* The Mercy of God
  The Miraculous Realm of God's Love
  The Outpouring of the Spirit—The Result of Prayer
* The Power of the Tongue
  The Power to Be Forever Free
  The Troublemaker
* The Winning Attitude
* Welcome to the Family
* You Are Healed!
  Your Right-Standing With God

*Available in Spanish

Books by Gloria Copeland

*   And Jesus Healed Them All
Are You Ready?
Build Yourself an Ark
Fight On!
From Faith to Faith—A Daily Guide to Victory
God's Prescription for Divine Health
God's Success Formula
God's Will for You
God's Will for Your Healing
God's Will Is Prosperity
God's Will Is the Holy Spirit
*   Harvest of Health
Healing Promises
Love—The Secret to Your Success
No Deposit—No Return
Pleasing the Father
Pressing In—It's Worth It All
The Power to Live a New Life
The Unbeatable Spirit of Faith
*   Walk in the Spirit
Walk With God
Well Worth the Wait

*Available in Spanish

Other Books Published by KCP

Heirs Together by Mac Hammond
John G. Lake—His Life, His Sermons, His Boldness of Faith
The New Testament in Modern Speech by Richard Francis Weymouth
Real People. Real Needs. Real Victories.
Winning the World by Mac Hammond

World Offices of
Kenneth Copeland Ministries

For more information about KCM and a free catalog, please write the office nearest you:

Kenneth Copeland Ministries
Fort Worth, Texas 76192-0001

Kenneth Copeland
Locked Bag 2600
Mansfield Delivery Centre
QUEENSLAND 4122
AUSTRALIA

Kenneth Copeland
Post Office Box 830
RANDBURG
2125
REPUBLIC OF SOUTH AFRICA

220123 MINSK
REPUBLIC OF BELARUS
Post Office 123
P/B 35
Kenneth Copeland Ministries

Kenneth Copeland
Post Office Box 15
BATH
BA1 1GD
ENGLAND

Kenneth Copeland
Post Office Box 378
Surrey
BRITISH COLUMBIA
V3T 5B6
CANADA